LADDERS *to* SUCCESS™

on the **CRCT**

LEVEL **E**

Mathematics

LEVELED INSTRUCTION AND PRACTICE ON 10 ESSENTIAL SKILLS

PHOTO CREDITS

Ladders to Success on the CRCT, Mathematics, Level E
101GA
ISBN-10: 1-59823-551-6
ISBN-13: 978-1-59823-551-7

Cover Illustration: Sam Ward/Mendola Artists

Triumph Learning® 136 Madison Avenue, 7th Floor, New York, NY 10016
A Haights Cross Communications, Inc. company

Table of Contents

Georgia Performance Standards

Letter to the Student

Dear Student,

Welcome to **Ladders to Success** for Level E. This book will help you work on the ten math skills most important to you this year. There is one lesson for each skill. You will master all ten skills by working through all ten lessons one by one.

This book does not rush you through a skill. Each lesson is fourteen pages long. This gives you plenty of time to really get comfortable learning what each skill means. You will see how each skill works in math problems.

The first page of every lesson is called Show What You Know. Take this short quiz to see how much you know about a skill before digging into the lesson. The next section, Guided Instruction 1, will start you off with some friendly guided review and practice. Practice the Skill 1, which follows Guided Instruction 1, shows you how to answer a multiple-choice question before asking you to try more by yourself. The next section, News Flash, is an exciting news story. It also comes with an activity.

Following the first News Flash is a three-page section called Ladder to Success. This section will give you three chances to practice the skill. Each practice is a little harder as you go "up the ladder." Now you are ready for the second part of the lesson.

The second part of the lesson is just like the first. You will see Guided Instruction 2, Practice the Skill 2, and another News Flash. This time around these sections are a little harder. The last two pages of each lesson are called Show What You Learned. Show off everything you have learned in the lesson by correctly answering multiple-choice questions on the skill. Words that are boldfaced in the lessons appear in the glossary at the back of the book.

The lessons in this book will help you practice and improve your skills. They will also get you ready for the tests you will be taking this year. Some of the practice will be in the style of the state test. You will be answering multiple-choice and open-ended questions. You may see questions like these on your state test. Practicing with these types of questions will build your confidence.

We hope you will enjoy using *Ladders to Success.* We want you to climb the ladder to success this year. This book will help you get started!

Letter to the Family

Dear Parent or Family Member,

The **Ladders to Success** series of workbooks is designed to prepare your child to master ten of the fundamental skills in mathematics that are essential for success, both in the curriculum and on state tests. *Ladders to Success* provides guided review and practice for the skills that are the building blocks of your child's education in math. These are also the skills that will be tested on the state test in mathematics. Your child's success will be measured by how well he or she masters these skills.

Ladders to Success is a unique program in that each lesson is organized to ensure your child's success. Ten skills that students often find challenging are treated individually in ten lessons. Students are guided and supported through the first part of each lesson until they are ready to take on unguided practice in the second part of the lesson. Each lesson is fourteen pages long to give the student ample opportunity to review and practice a skill until a comfort level is reached. Support is gradually withdrawn throughout the lesson to build your child's confidence for independent work at the end of each lesson.

We invite you to be our partner in making learning a priority in your child's life. To help ensure success, we suggest that you review the lessons in this book with your child. You will see how each lesson gets subtly but progressively harder as you go along. While teachers will guide your child through the book in class, your support at home, added to the support of guided instruction and practice in the series, is vital to your child's comprehension.

We ask you to work with us this year to help your young student climb the ladder to success. Together, we can make a difference!

Letter to the Teacher

Dear Teacher,

Welcome to **Ladders to Success** on the CRCT in Mathematics for Level E. The Ladders to Success series of workbooks for mathematics is designed to prepare your students to master ten fundamental, grade-appropriate skills in math that are essential for success, both in the curriculum and on your state tests. Ladders provides guided review and practice for the skills that are the building blocks of the student's education. These are also skills that will be tested on your state tests in mathematics.

Ladders to Success is a unique program in that each lesson is leveled, or scaffolded, to ensure your students' success. Students are guided and supported through the first part of each lesson until they are ready to take on unguided practice in the second part of the lesson. Ten important skills are treated individually in ten lessons. Each lesson is fourteen pages long to give the student ample opportunity to review and practice a skill until a comfort level is reached. Support is slowly withdrawn throughout the lesson to build your students' confidence for independent work at the end of each lesson.

Ladders has a consistent, symmetrical format. The format is predictable from lesson to lesson, which increases students' comfort level with the presentation of skills-based information and practice. The first page of every lesson is called Show What You Know. This is a short diagnostic quiz to determine how much a student knows about a particular skill before digging into the lesson. It represents a snapshot of where each student is "now" before additional review and practice. This diagnostic quiz can be your guide in the way you choose to use the different parts of the lesson that follows.

The next section, Guided Instruction 1, will start students off slowly with guided review and practice. Practice the Skill 1, which immediately follows Guided Instruction 1, models how to answer a multiple-choice question before asking students to try more by themselves. The next section, News Flash, is an exciting contemporary news story that will engage students' interest. It is accompanied by an activity, often involving a math tool, under the heading Solve It.

Following the first News Flash is a three-page section called Ladder to Success, which embodies the spirit of the Ladders series. This section provides three more chances to practice the skill. What makes this section unique is that each practice is a little harder as students go "up the ladder." By the time students have finished the third practice, they are ready for the second part of the lesson, which mirrors the first part. The Ladder to Success section is the crucial bridge between the first part of the lesson and the second.

Thus, you will now see Guided Instruction 2, Practice the Skill 2, and another News Flash. This time around, however, these sections are more challenging. The problems are more difficult, and there is less modeling. The activity under the Solve It heading in the second News Flash in each lesson, for example, is an unscaffolded math activity.

The last two pages of each lesson represent a Posttest on the skill of the lesson. It is called Show What You Learned. This is the student's chance to show off everything he or she learned in the lesson by successfully answering multiple-choice questions on the skill. The Posttest ends with an open-ended question, giving students the opportunity to show a deeper understanding of the skill now that they have completed the lesson. Words that are boldfaced in the lessons appear in the glossary at the back of the book.

Triumph Learning supports you in the difficult challenges you face in engaging your students in the learning process. *Ladders to Success* attempts to address some of these challenges by providing lessons that contain interesting material; scaffolded, or leveled, support; and a spectrum of multiple-choice questions and open-ended activities. This will allow students to build their confidence as they work toward proficiency with each skill in each lesson.

We ask you to work with us this year to help your students climb the ladder to success. Together, we *will* make a difference!

Show What You Know

M5N3.c.   Multiply and divide with decimals including decimals less than one and greater than one.

Before you begin this lesson on decimal operations, answer these questions. Choose the letter of the correct answer for each problem. Round your answer to the nearest hundredth, when necessary.

1. $8 \times 0.6 = \boxed{}$

   What is the product?

   A 0.48

   B 4.8

   C 48.0

   D 480.0

2. $5.2 \div 4 = \boxed{}$

   What is the quotient?

   A 0.01

   B 0.13

   C 1.30

   D 13.00

3.   4.3
    $\times 7.2$

   What is the product?

   A 28.6

   B 29.26

   C 30.96

   D 41.7

4. $125.52 \div 52.3 = \boxed{}$

   What is the quotient?

   A 2.4

   B 2.04

   C 0.24

   D 0.02

5. A zookeeper measured a newborn animal and found it was 3.2 centimeters long. Five weeks later the zookeeper measured the animal again, and found it was 17.6 centimeters long. How many times longer is the animal at 5 weeks than when it was born?

   A 3.8 times longer

   B 4.3 times longer

   C 5.2 times longer

   D 5.5 times longer

6. Caroline earns $9.75 an hour. How much money will she earn if she works 22.5 hours in 1 week?

   A $219.38

   B $206.96

   C $87.75

   D $21.94

LESSON
1
Decimal Operations

Guided Instruction 1

M5N3.c. Multiply and divide with decimals including decimals less than one and greater than one.

Introduction

When you multiply **decimals** by whole numbers, you find the **product** of two or more groups that are the same size. You will first study how to multiply a decimal by a whole number using models.

Here's How

What is 7 × 0.4?

Think About It

You can use 10-by-1 grids to model multiplying a decimal by a whole number. Each 10-by-1 grid represents 1 whole.

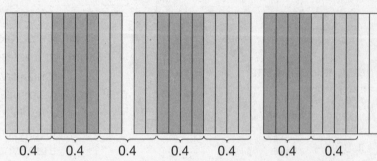

0.4   0.4   0.4   0.4   0.4   0.4   0.4

Count how many grids are completely shaded. This is the whole number part of your product.

Count how many columns in the last grid are shaded. This is the decimal part of your product.

So, 7 × 0.4 = 2.8.

Try This Strategy

Use Paper and Pencil

You can multiply decimals using the same strategies you use to multiply whole numbers.

What is 0.9 × 3?

```
  0.9   ← 1 place
× 3     ← 0 places
─────
  2.7   ← Count 1 place from
          the right to place the
          decimal point.
```

To place the decimal point in the product, count the total number of digits after the decimal point in each factor.

Then, count in that many places from the right of the product to place the decimal point.

Study the problem. Use the **Math Guide** for tips that can help you understand how to divide a decimal by a whole number to find the **quotient**.

Math Guide	
Rewrite the problem using a division house.	What is 19.8 ÷ 5?
Place the **decimal point** in the quotient above the decimal point in the **dividend**.	$5\overline{)19.8}$
Divide as with whole numbers. Add zeros, as needed, to the dividend, to continue to divide.	$\begin{array}{r} 3.96 \\ 5\overline{)19.80} \\ -15 \\ \hline 48 \\ -45 \\ \hline 30 \end{array}$
Use multiplication to check your solution.	$\begin{array}{r} 3.96 \\ \times5 \\ \hline 19.80 \end{array}$ So, 19.8 ÷ 5 = 3.96.

Now use what you already know and what you learned to multiply and divide with decimals.

Answer the questions on the next page.

Practice the Skill 1

M5N3.c.   Multiply and divide with decimals including decimals less than one and greater than one.

Practice multiplying and dividing with decimals by solving the problems below.

EXAMPLE

$10.5 \div 7 = \boxed{}$

What is the quotient?

   A 0.02
   B 0.15
   C 1.5
   D 15.0

What do you need to find?

Find the quotient of $10.5 \div 7$.

Place the decimal point in the quotient.

Then, divide as you would with whole numbers.

$$
\begin{array}{r}
1.5 \\
7\overline{)10.5} \\
-7\downarrow \\
\hline
35 \\
-35 \\
\hline
0
\end{array}
$$

What is the quotient?

1.5

Now read each question. Circle the letter of the correct answer.

1. $4 \times 0.8 = \boxed{}$

What is the product?

   A 320.0
   B 32.0
   C 3.2
   D 0.32

2. $50.4 \div 14 = \boxed{}$

What is the quotient?

   A 3.2
   B 3.6
   C 30.2
   D 36.0

3. $21 \times 0.6 = \boxed{}$

What is the product?

   A 0.126
   B 1.26
   C 12.6
   D 126.0

4. $18\overline{)64.8}$

What is the quotient?

   A 4.8
   B 3.6
   C 0.48
   D 0.36

Cosmonauts Touch Down in Classrooms

Danville, VA—Two Russian cosmonauts visited students. to talk with them about space technology. Cosmonaut is the Russian word for astronaut.

One of the visitors, Yury Usachev, has been on four trips to space—including trips to the International Space Station (ISS). Usachev told students that to be a cosmonaut, a person has to be ready for anything. The person also needs to know the job is dangerous. He also said that it is very important to have excellent math and science skills.

Usachev showed students pictures of what life is like in the weightless conditions of space. The pictures showed him brushing his teeth with a floating toothbrush, washing his face with a ball of bouncing water, and exercising while tied to the floor!

Solve It

Imagine you are finding out more about what it is like to be a cosmonaut. Show your work on a separate sheet of paper.

1. One cosmonaut spends 80 days in space. He spends 0.4 of those days in the ISS. How many days does he spend in the ISS?

2. There are 25 cosmonauts prepared for a trip to the ISS. For one trip to the ISS, 3 cosmonauts are selected to go. What decimal represents the number of cosmonauts selected to go to the ISS out of the 25 cosmonauts?

LADDERS to SUCCESS

LESSON
1
Decimal Operations

M5N3.c.   Multiply and divide with decimals including decimals less than one and greater than one.

Ladder to Success

Review

You have learned how to multiply and divide with decimals.

Review the methods you can use to multiply and divide with decimals.

- You can use 10-by-1 grids to model decimal multiplication.
- You can use paper and pencil to solve decimal multiplication and decimal division problems.

Practice 1

Sophia runs 0.8 mile on Monday, Wednesday, Thursday, and Saturday. She does not run any other days during the week. How many miles does she run in 1 week?

What I Already Know	Sophia runs 0.8 of a mile each time she runs. She runs 4 days (Monday, Wednesday, Thursday, and Saturday) each week.
What I Need to Find Out	How many miles does she run in one week?
What I Need to Do	Multiply 0.8 by 4.

You can use 10-by-1 grids to solve the problem. Shade the grids to show 4 × 0.8.

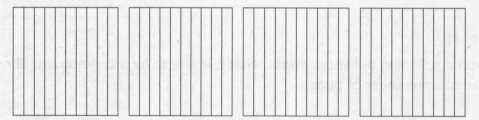

How many miles does Sophia run each week? _____

---

1. 0.3 × 24 = ☐

What is the product?

A 7.2   **C** 0.62

B 6.2   **D** 0.72

2. 0.9 × 12 = ☐

What is the product?

A 0.18   **C** 9.8

B 0.98   **D** 10.8

Practice 2

In science class, Rory measures a centipede. It is 3.2 centimeters long and has 16 segments. If each segment is the same length, how long is each segment?

What I Already Know	The centipede is 3.2 centimeters long. The centipede has 16 segments.
What I Need to Find Out	How long is each segment?
What I Need to Do	Divide 3.2 by 16.

Since you need to divide a decimal by a whole number, you can use paper and pencil.

Complete the division problem.

$$16\overline{)3.2}$$

How long is each segment of the centipede? _____

How can you check your work? _____

Show how to check your work in the space below.

---

1. $6.3 \div 2 = \boxed{}$

What is the quotient?

A 31.5

B 3.15

C 0.32

D 0.03

2. $9.4 \div 5 = \boxed{}$

What is the quotient?

A 1.08

B 1.80

C 1.88

D 18.8

Practice 3

Jack has two 30-inch pieces of rope. He needs to cut one 30-inch piece of rope into 4 equal pieces. He needs to cut the other 30-inch piece of rope into 8 equal pieces. How long will each piece of the ropes be after they are cut? Show your answers as decimals.

Reread the problem to see what you need to do.

You need to find out how long each piece of rope will be. This means you should divide 30 by 4 and 30 by 8 to find the answers.

How can you divide to find the answers?

You can divide using paper and pencil. To show your answer as a decimal, place the decimal point to the right of the ones digit in the quotient and dividend. Then, add zeros to the dividend to continue dividing.

Examine the division of 30 by 4.

```
       7.5
   4)30.0
   – 28 ↓
       2 0
     – 2 0
         0
```

Now complete the division of 30 by 8 on your own.

```
8)30
```

How long is each piece of rope if the rope is cut into 4 equal pieces?

_____

How long is each piece of rope if the rope is cut into 8 equal pieces?

_____

LESSON
1
Decimal Operations

Guided Instruction 2

M5N3.c.   Multiply and divide with decimals including decimals less than one and greater than one.

You will build upon what you learned in Part 1 by learning to multiply and divide decimals by decimals.

What is 0.5 × 0.3?

Think About It

You can use 10-by-10 grids to model multiplying a decimal by a decimal. Each 10-by-10 grid represents 1 whole.

First, shade columns to show 0.5, the first factor.	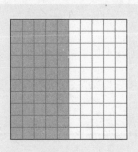	Then, shade rows to show 0.3, the second factor. 

Count the squares that are shaded twice. That is the product.

So, 0.5 × 0.3 = 0.15.

Use Paper and Pencil

Multiply as with whole numbers. Then, count the number of decimal places in the factors to place the decimal point in the product.

What is 3.25 × 2.1?

```
    3.25   ←  2 places
  × 2.1    ←  1 place
    325
   6500
   6.825   ←  Count 3 places from the right to place the decimal point.
```

Study the problem. Use the **Math Guide** for tips that can help you understand how to divide a decimal by a decimal.

 Math Guide

Multiply the **divisor** and dividend by a power of 10 to make the divisor a whole number.

What is 9.9 ÷ 3.25? Round your answer to the nearest hundredth.

$$3.25.\overline{)9.90.}$$
$$\times 100 \quad \times 100$$

Divide as with whole numbers.

Divide to one place further than you want to round to.

$$\begin{array}{r} 3.046 \\ 325\overline{)990.000} \\ -\ 975\ \\ \hline 1500 \\ -\ 1300 \\ \hline 2000 \end{array}$$

Use rounding rules to round to the nearest hundredth.

3.046 rounds to 3.05.

So, 9.9 ÷ 3.25 to the nearest hundredth is 3.05.

Now use what you already know and what you learned to multiply and divide with decimals.

Answer the questions on the next page.

Practice the Skill 2

LESSON 1

Decimal Operations

M5N3.c. Multiply and divide with decimals including decimals less than one and greater than one.

LADDERS to SUCCESS

Choose the correct answer. Round your answer to the nearest hundredth, when necessary.

1. $0.6 \times 0.4 = \square$

   What is the product?

   A 0.024
   B 0.24
   C 2.4
   D 24.0

2. $62.4 \div 0.89 = \square$

   What is the quotient?

   A 71.0
   B 70.11
   C 7.01
   D 0.71

3. Cho earns $8.15 each hour. If she works 9.5 hours, how much money will she earn?

   A $77.01
   B $77.33
   C $77.43
   D $88.10

4. $0.43 \div 0.6 = \square$

   What is the quotient?

   A 0.72
   B 0.75
   C 7.17
   D 7.20

5. Miguel purchased 1.8 pounds of bananas for $1.25. How much did Miguel pay per pound for the bananas?

   A $0.69
   B $0.70
   C $1.13
   D $2.25

6. Kara bought 2.5 pounds of peaches for $2.30 per pound. How much did Kara spend on the peaches?

   A $1.61
   B $5.62
   C $5.65
   D $5.75

Chicago, IL—This Valentine's Day instead of giving chocolate hearts, competitive eaters ate the chocolate hearts themselves! The night before Valentine's Day competitive eaters gathered in Chicago, Illinois, to eat as many 3.5-ounce chocolate hearts as possible in 7 minutes.

About 3 minutes into the contest, competitor Patrick Bertoletti ran out of the warm water he had been sipping between bites to help soften the chocolate. He had to use cold water instead. Even with this problem, Bertoletti still won the competition. He ate about 7 ounces more chocolate than the second-place finisher!

Eating Your Heart Out ...in Chocolate

Solve It

Answer the questions. Show your work on a separate sheet of paper.

1. One contestant was able to finish 5.25 of the 3.5-ounce chocolate hearts during the competition. How many ounces of chocolate did the contestant eat? Round your answer to the nearest hundredth.

_____

2. Patrick Bertoletti ate 31.5 ounces of chocolate to win the competition. Each chocolate heart weighed 3.5 ounces. How many chocolate hearts did Bertoletti eat?

_____

Show What You Learned

M5N3.c.   Multiply and divide with decimals including decimals less than one and greater than one.

Now that you have practiced decimal operations, take this quiz to show what you have learned. Choose the letter of the correct answer for each problem. Round your answer to the nearest hundredth, when necessary.

1. Janna has 6 pieces of cord. Each piece of cord is 0.8 inches long. How much cord does Janna have in all?

   A 0.05 in.

   B 0.48 in.

   C 4.8 in.

   D 48.0 in.

2. Ken measures an insect that is 4.2 cm long. The insect has 3 body segments that are each the same size. How long is each segment?

   A 0.14 cm

   B 1.06 cm

   C 1.4 cm

   D 1.6 cm

3.   8.23
      $\times$ 4.9

   What is the product?

   A 40.03

   B 40.11

   C 40.32

   D 40.33

4. A costume maker has 27 inches of ribbon. She cuts it into 6 equal pieces. How many inches long is each piece of ribbon?

   A 4.5 in.

   B 4.2 in.

   C 3.5 in.

   D 3.3 in.

5. $0.8 \times 0.9 = \boxed{}$

   What is the product?

   A 0.07

   B 0.72

   C 7.2

   D 72.0

6. Simon's puppy weighed 1.2 pounds when it was born. The puppy now weighs 10.5 pounds. How many times heavier is the puppy now compared to when it was born?

   A 8.75 times heavier

   B 8.80 times heavier

   C 8.85 times heavier

   D 8.90 times heavier

7. 12.5 ÷ 3 = ☐

What is the quotient?

A 4.17

B 4.21

C 41.67

D 42.13

8. Paul gets $0.08 change when he buys his lunch each day. If he saves all of his change from lunch, how much money will he have after 30 days?

A $0.24

B $2.40

C $24.00

D $24.24

9. 1.2)‾3.58‾

What is the quotient?

A 31.50

B 29.83

C 3.15

D 2.98

10. Sierra buys 2.3 pounds of smoked turkey for $2.19 per pound. How much does she pay for the turkey in all?

A $5.04

B $4.94

C $4.51

D $1.09

11. Sierra also buys Swiss cheese. She pays $1.79 for 0.6 of a pound of Swiss cheese. How much does the Swiss cheese cost per pound?

A $1.07

B $1.19

C $2.87

D $2.98

Show your work on a separate sheet of paper.

12. Omar earns $9.20 per hour. If he works 6.5 hours in 1 week, how much money will he earn that week? Show your work and explain how you know where to place the decimal point in your answer.

Show What You Know

M5N4.f.   Use $<$, $>$, or $=$ to compare fractions and justify the comparison.

Before you begin this lesson on comparing and ordering fractions, answer these questions. Choose the letter of the correct answer for each problem.

1. $\frac{2}{5} \bigcirc \frac{4}{5}$

   Which symbol completes the number sentence above?

   A $>$

   B $<$

   C $=$

   D $+$

2. Which fraction is equivalent to $\frac{3}{4}$?

   A $\frac{4}{5}$

   B $\frac{6}{9}$

   C $\frac{9}{16}$

   D $\frac{12}{16}$

3. $\frac{5}{8} \bigcirc \frac{7}{16}$

   Which symbol completes the number sentence above?

   A $>$

   B $<$

   C $=$

   D $+$

4. Which set of fractions below is ordered from greatest to least?

   A $\frac{1}{2}, \frac{2}{3}, \frac{1}{4}$

   B $\frac{2}{3}, \frac{1}{4}, \frac{1}{2}$

   C $\frac{2}{3}, \frac{1}{2}, \frac{1}{4}$

   D $\frac{1}{4}, \frac{2}{3}, \frac{1}{2}$

5. Mr. Jones has measuring cups for $\frac{1}{2}$ cup, $\frac{3}{4}$ cup, and $\frac{1}{3}$ cup. How are these measurements ordered from least to greatest?

   A $\frac{1}{2}$ cup, $\frac{3}{4}$ cup, $\frac{1}{3}$ cup

   B $\frac{3}{4}$ cup, $\frac{1}{2}$ cup, $\frac{1}{3}$ cup

   C $\frac{1}{3}$ cup, $\frac{1}{2}$ cup, $\frac{3}{4}$ cup

   D $\frac{1}{2}$ cup, $\frac{1}{3}$ cup, $\frac{3}{4}$ cup

6. In 5 minutes, Josiah ran $\frac{3}{8}$ of a mile, Kelli ran $\frac{1}{2}$ of a mile, Aidan ran $\frac{5}{16}$ of a mile, and Dawna ran $\frac{1}{4}$ of a mile. Who ran the least distance?

   A Josiah

   B Kelli

   C Aidan

   D Dawna

LESSON
2
Comparing and
Ordering Fractions

Guided Instruction 1

M5N4.f.   Use <, >, or = to compare fractions and justify the comparison.

When you compare two **fractions**, you decide which is greater or which is less. In Part 1, you will study how to compare fractions using models.

Here's How

Which fraction is greater, $\frac{3}{8}$ or $\frac{5}{8}$?

Think About It

Compare the fractions to determine which fraction is greater. You can use fraction strips to show each fraction.

| $\frac{1}{8}$ | $\frac{1}{8}$ | $\frac{1}{8}$ | $\frac{3}{8}$ |

| $\frac{1}{8}$ | $\frac{1}{8}$ | $\frac{1}{8}$ | $\frac{1}{8}$ | $\frac{1}{8}$ | $\frac{5}{8}$ |

Remember: > means greater than and < means less than.

Compare the fraction strips. Can you see why $\frac{3}{8} < \frac{5}{8}$? The fraction strips compare the size of each fraction and show that $\frac{5}{8}$ is greater than $\frac{3}{8}$.

So, $\frac{5}{8} > \frac{3}{8}$.

Try This Strategy

Compare Numerators

If two fractions have the same **denominator**, compare their **numerators**. The fraction with the greater numerator is the greater fraction.

Can you see why $\frac{7}{8} > \frac{3}{8}$?

Since 7 is greater than 3, $\frac{7}{8}$ is greater than $\frac{3}{8}$.

Study the problem. Use the Math Guide for tips that can help you understand how to compare fractions.

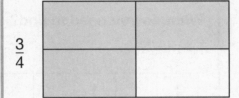

![Math Guide protractor icon] **Math Guide**

How are the fractions $\frac{3}{4}$, $\frac{1}{4}$, and $\frac{1}{2}$ ordered from least to greatest?

Notice you need to show the fractions from *least to greatest* or from *greatest to least*.

$\frac{3}{4}$

The three fractions have two different denominators. So, you cannot simply compare their numerators. Instead, model each fraction.

$\frac{1}{4}$

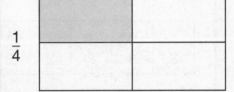

$\frac{1}{2}$

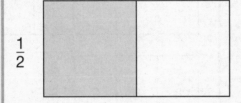

To order fractions, compare them two at a time.

- The model for $\frac{1}{4}$ has less shaded area than the model for $\frac{1}{2}$.

- The model for $\frac{1}{2}$ has less shaded area than the model for $\frac{3}{4}$.

Then use the comparisons to order all three fractions.

So, the fractions are ordered as $\frac{1}{4}$, $\frac{1}{2}$, $\frac{3}{4}$ from least to greatest.

Now use what you already know and what you learned to compare fractions.

Answer the questions on the next page.

Practice the Skill 1

M5N4.f.   Use <, >, or = to compare fractions and justify the comparison.

Practice comparing and ordering fractions by solving the problems below.

EXAMPLE

Which fraction is the greatest?

A $\frac{5}{8}$

B $\frac{7}{8}$

C $\frac{3}{4}$

D $\frac{3}{8}$

What do you need to find?

Find the greatest fraction using fraction strips.

| $\frac{1}{8}$ | $\frac{1}{8}$ | $\frac{1}{8}$ | $\frac{1}{8}$ | $\frac{1}{8}$ | $\frac{5}{8}$ |

| $\frac{1}{8}$ | $\frac{1}{8}$ | $\frac{1}{8}$ | $\frac{1}{8}$ | $\frac{1}{8}$ | $\frac{1}{8}$ | $\frac{1}{8}$ | $\frac{7}{8}$ |

| $\frac{1}{4}$ | $\frac{1}{4}$ | $\frac{1}{4}$ | $\frac{3}{4}$ |

| $\frac{1}{8}$ | $\frac{1}{8}$ | $\frac{1}{8}$ | $\frac{3}{8}$ |

Now read each question. Circle the letter of the best answer. You may use fraction strips.

1. Compare $\frac{3}{5}$ and $\frac{1}{5}$. Which number sentence is true?

    A $\frac{3}{5} = \frac{1}{5}$

    B $\frac{3}{5} < \frac{1}{5}$

    C $\frac{3}{5} > \frac{1}{5}$

    D $\frac{3}{5} + \frac{1}{5}$

2. How are $\frac{1}{10}, \frac{7}{10}, \frac{3}{10}$, and 1 ordered from greatest to least?

    A $1, \frac{1}{10}, \frac{3}{10}, \frac{7}{10}$

    B $\frac{1}{10}, \frac{3}{10}, \frac{7}{10}, 1$

    C $\frac{7}{10}, \frac{3}{10}, \frac{1}{10}, 1$

    D $1, \frac{7}{10}, \frac{3}{10}, \frac{1}{10}$

NEWS FLASH!

World's Best Eaters Compete in Hot Dog Eating Contest

Brooklyn, NY—People watched as eaters quickly stuffed hot dogs into their mouths! Twenty eaters from around the world came to Coney Island for the International Hot Dog Eating Contest. They ate as many hot dogs as they could in 12 minutes. The winner took home the Mustard Yellow International Belt, the greatest prize in competitive eating. Takeru Kobayashi won for the fifth year in a row. The 27-year-old from Japan ate 49 hot dogs. That's more than four hot dogs a minute! This is not the only eating contest Kobayashi has won. In another contest he ate 57 cow brains in 15 minutes!

Solve It

Now you will apply the skill to real life. What if you went to see a hot dog eating contest? Show your work on a separate sheet of paper.

1. Tom ate $\frac{2}{3}$ of a hot dog in one minute. Louise ate $\frac{1}{3}$ of a hot dog in one minute. Who ate more in one minute?

Lu was able to eat 10 hot dogs in $\frac{1}{3}$ hour. Pia ate 10 hot dogs in $\frac{1}{5}$ hour and Jose ate 10 hot dogs in $\frac{1}{4}$ hour.

2. Who took the most time to eat 10 hot dogs?

3. Order the times from least to greatest.

Ladder to Success

M5N4.f.   Use <, >, or = to compare fractions and justify the comparison.

Review

You have learned how to compare fractions.

Review the steps you can use to compare fractions.

- If two fractions have the same denominator, use fraction strips or compare their numerators.

- If two fractions have different denominators, draw models to "see" the amounts.

Practice 1

Janine measures the growth of plants each week for a science experiment. This week, a cactus grew $\frac{3}{8}$ inch and a zinnia plant grew $\frac{5}{8}$ inch. Which plant grew more?

What I Already Know	A cactus grew $\frac{3}{8}$ inch and a zinnia plant grew $\frac{5}{8}$ inch.
What I Need to Find Out	Which plant grew more?
What I Need to Do	Compare $\frac{3}{8}$ and $\frac{5}{8}$.

Since $\frac{3}{8}$ and $\frac{5}{8}$ have the same denominator, use models to compare the numerators.

Draw models to show $\frac{3}{8}$ and $\frac{5}{8}$.

Use the models to complete the statement. $\frac{3}{8}$ ◯ $\frac{5}{8}$

Which plant grew more? _____

---

1. Which number sentence is true?

   A $\frac{7}{12} = \frac{5}{12}$

   B $\frac{7}{12} < \frac{5}{12}$

   C $\frac{7}{12} > \frac{5}{12}$

   D $\frac{7}{12} + \frac{5}{12}$

2. $\frac{3}{6}$ ◯ $\frac{5}{6}$

   Which symbol completes the number sentence?

   A =

   B <

   C >

   D +

Practice 2

Janine is growing two pepper seedlings. This week the serrano seedling grew $\frac{3}{4}$ inch and the Anaheim seedling grew $\frac{9}{16}$ inch. Which seedling grew more this week?

What I Already Know	A serrano seedling grew $\frac{3}{4}$ inch and the Anaheim seedling grew $\frac{9}{16}$ inch.
What I Need to Find Out	Which seedling grew more?
What I Need to Do	Compare $\frac{3}{4}$ and $\frac{9}{16}$.

Since $\frac{3}{4}$ and $\frac{9}{16}$ have different denominators, use a number line to compare the fractions.

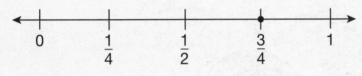

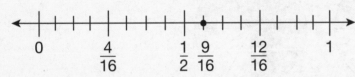

Which seedling grew more? _____

How can you tell? _____

_____

---

1. Which number sentence is true?

   A $\frac{1}{3} = \frac{1}{4}$

   B $\frac{1}{3} < \frac{1}{4}$

   C $\frac{1}{3} > \frac{1}{4}$

   D $\frac{1}{3} + \frac{1}{4}$

2. $\frac{5}{12} \bigcirc \frac{3}{4}$

   Which symbol completes the number sentence above?

   A =

   B <

   C >

   D +

Practice 3

Kenji measures the length of two insects. He finds that insect A is $\frac{3}{4}$ inch long and insect B is $\frac{2}{3}$ inch long. Which insect is longer?

Reread the problem to see what you need to do.

You need to find out which insect is longer. That means you should compare $\frac{3}{4}$ and $\frac{2}{3}$, and then choose the greater fraction.

How can you compare $\frac{3}{4}$ and $\frac{2}{3}$?

Their denominators are different. You could use fraction strips to solve this problem. Another way to compare fractions with different denominators is to use a common denominator.

Examine the rewriting of $\frac{3}{4}$ below.

$$\frac{3}{4} = \frac{3 \times 3}{4 \times 3} = \frac{9}{12}$$

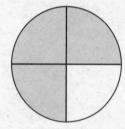 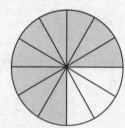

Now complete the rewriting of $\frac{2}{3}$ on your own.

$$\frac{2}{3} = \frac{2 \times \bigcirc}{3 \times \bigcirc} = \frac{\bigcirc}{12}$$

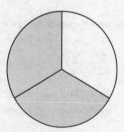 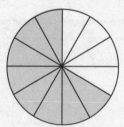

So, which insect is longer? _____

How can you tell? _____

_____

Guided Instruction 2

M5N4.f. Use $<$, $>$, or $=$ to compare fractions and justify the comparison.

To compare and order fractions with different denominators in Part 2, you will use the idea of **equivalent fractions**.

Here's How

Order the fractions $\frac{5}{6}$, $\frac{1}{4}$, and $\frac{2}{3}$ from least to greatest.

Think About It

The three fractions have three different denominators, making them hard to compare. You can use the least common denominator to solve this problem.

Find the least common denominator by listing the multiples of each denominator.

Multiples of 6: 6, (12), 18, 24, 30, 36, 42

Multiples of 4: 4, 8, (12), 16, 20, 24, 28

Multiples of 3: 3, 6, 9, (12), 15, 18, 21

For the denominators 6, 4, and 3, the least common denominator is 12.

$\frac{5}{6} = \frac{5 \times 2}{6 \times 2} = \frac{10}{12}$	$\frac{1}{4} = \frac{1 \times 3}{4 \times 3} = \frac{3}{12}$	$\frac{2}{3} = \frac{2 \times 4}{3 \times 4} = \frac{8}{12}$

Once the equivalent fractions with denominator of 12 are written, they are easy to compare and order using the three numerators.

Since $\frac{3}{12} < \frac{8}{12} < \frac{10}{12}$, the fractions ordered from least to greatest are $\frac{1}{4}, \frac{2}{3}, \frac{5}{6}$.

Try This Strategy

Draw a Number Line

You can use a 0 to 1 number line to order the fractions from least to greatest by reading them from left to right.

Study the problem. Use the **Math Guide** for tips that can help you understand how to compare mixed numbers using a number line.

<table>
<tr><td>📐 **Math Guide**</td><td>Theo ran on four mornings this week. He ran $3\frac{3}{4}$ miles on Monday, $2\frac{1}{2}$ miles on Wednesday, $2\frac{3}{4}$ miles on Thursday, and $3\frac{1}{4}$ miles on Friday. Order Theo's distances from least to greatest.</td></tr>
<tr><td>You can use a number line to compare **mixed numbers**.</td><td>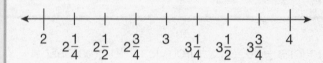</td></tr>
<tr><td>Identify the whole number in a mixed number.</td><td>$3\frac{3}{4}$ is between 3 and 4 on the number line.</td></tr>
<tr><td>Locate and label the mixed number.</td><td>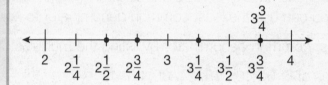</td></tr>
<tr><td>Label each mixed number on the number line.</td><td>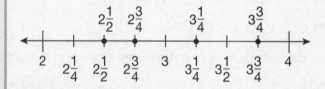</td></tr>
<tr><td>Fractions on a number line are shown least to greatest from left to right.</td><td>Theo's distances in order from least to greatest are: $2\frac{1}{2}$ miles, $2\frac{3}{4}$ miles, $3\frac{1}{4}$ miles, $3\frac{3}{4}$ miles.</td></tr>
</table>

Now use what you already know and what you learned to order fractions.

Answer the questions on the next page.

Practice the Skill 2

M5N4.f.   Use $<$, $>$, or $=$ to compare fractions and justify the comparison.

Choose the correct answer. Use the information in problem 1 for problems 1–3.

1. The Walking Club walked four days this week. Its members walked $2\frac{1}{4}$ miles on Monday, $1\frac{3}{8}$ miles on Wednesday, $2\frac{1}{8}$ miles on Friday, and $1\frac{3}{4}$ miles on Saturday. On which day did the Walking Club walk the least distance?

   A Monday

   B Wednesday

   C Friday

   D Saturday

2. On which day did the Walking Club walk the greatest distance?

   A Monday

   B Wednesday

   C Friday

   D Saturday

3. Which shows the Walking Club's distances ordered from greatest to least?

   A $1\frac{3}{4}$ mi., $1\frac{3}{8}$ mi., $2\frac{1}{4}$ mi., $2\frac{1}{8}$ mi.

   B $1\frac{3}{8}$ mi., $1\frac{3}{4}$ mi., $2\frac{1}{8}$ mi., $2\frac{1}{4}$ mi.

   C $2\frac{1}{4}$ mi., $2\frac{1}{8}$ mi., $1\frac{3}{4}$ mi., $1\frac{3}{8}$ mi.

   D $2\frac{1}{4}$ mi., $2\frac{1}{8}$ mi., $1\frac{3}{8}$ mi., $1\frac{3}{4}$ mi.

4. Which statement is true?

   A $\frac{7}{9} < \frac{5}{7}$

   B $\frac{7}{9} > \frac{5}{7}$

   C $\frac{7}{9} = \frac{5}{7}$

   D $\frac{7}{9} + \frac{5}{7}$

5. Which shows the fractions $\frac{1}{5}$, $\frac{2}{11}$, and $\frac{3}{10}$ ordered from greatest to least?

   A $\frac{1}{5}$, $\frac{2}{11}$, $\frac{3}{10}$

   B $\frac{1}{5}$, $\frac{3}{10}$, $\frac{2}{11}$

   C $\frac{3}{10}$, $\frac{1}{5}$, $\frac{2}{11}$

   D $\frac{2}{11}$, $\frac{1}{5}$, $\frac{3}{10}$

6. Which shows the mixed numbers $3\frac{2}{3}$, $3\frac{1}{5}$, and $2\frac{4}{5}$ ordered from least to greatest?

   A $3\frac{1}{5}$, $3\frac{2}{3}$, $2\frac{4}{5}$

   B $2\frac{4}{5}$, $3\frac{1}{5}$, $3\frac{2}{3}$

   C $2\frac{4}{5}$, $3\frac{2}{3}$, $3\frac{1}{5}$

   D $3\frac{2}{3}$, $3\frac{1}{5}$, $2\frac{4}{5}$

NEWS FLASH!

BUG DINNER YUM!

Ames, IA—Scientists at Iowa State University think that eating bugs may be better for you than eating meat or fish. Properly prepared, bugs can be very healthful. They contain vitamins and protein and other good stuff.

People all over the world have eaten bugs for hundreds of years. In Algeria, people used to cook desert insects in the sun. In Australia, people collected beehives not only to gather the honey, but also to eat the bees. Bugs have been eaten in Japan for a long time. Some Japanese restaurants serve bug meals today.

Many people in the United States think bug eating is gross, but not everyone. Students at Iowa State University have come up with their own tasty bug recipes. Their "Banana Worm Bread" calls for $\frac{3}{8}$ cup of worms. To make "Chocolate Chirpie Chip Cookies," you need $\frac{1}{2}$ cup of crickets. You can even make grasshopper pizza by tossing $\frac{1}{4}$ cup of insects on your pie. With so many vitamins in bugs, these treats may be the healthful answer to junk food!

Solve It

1. Shade the rectangles below to show the three fractions from the story.

2. Order $\frac{3}{8}$, $\frac{1}{2}$, and $\frac{1}{4}$ from least to greatest.

Show What You Learned

M5N4.f.   Use $<$, $>$, or $=$ to compare fractions and justify the comparison.

Now that you have practiced comparing and ordering fractions, take this quiz to show what you learned. Choose the letter of the correct answer for each problem.

1. Which number sentence is true?

   A $\dfrac{1}{3} > \dfrac{2}{3}$

   B $\dfrac{1}{3} < \dfrac{2}{3}$

   C $\dfrac{1}{3} = \dfrac{2}{3}$

   D $\dfrac{1}{3} + \dfrac{2}{3}$

2. Which number sentence is true?

   A $\dfrac{2}{7} > \dfrac{2}{11}$

   B $\dfrac{2}{7} < \dfrac{2}{11}$

   C $\dfrac{2}{7} = \dfrac{2}{11}$

   D $\dfrac{2}{7} + \dfrac{2}{11}$

3. Which number sentence is true?

   A $\dfrac{6}{8} < \dfrac{9}{12}$

   B $\dfrac{6}{8} > \dfrac{9}{12}$

   C $\dfrac{6}{8} = \dfrac{9}{12}$

   D $\dfrac{6}{8} + \dfrac{9}{12}$

4. Which set of fractions is ordered from least to greatest?

   A $\dfrac{1}{2}, \dfrac{1}{3}, \dfrac{2}{3}, \dfrac{1}{4}$

   B $\dfrac{2}{3}, \dfrac{1}{2}, \dfrac{1}{3}, \dfrac{1}{4}$

   C $\dfrac{1}{4}, \dfrac{1}{3}, \dfrac{2}{3}, \dfrac{1}{2}$

   D $\dfrac{1}{4}, \dfrac{1}{3}, \dfrac{1}{2}, \dfrac{2}{3}$

5. Which set of mixed numbers is ordered from greatest to least?

   A $7\dfrac{1}{5}, 7\dfrac{1}{10}, 6\dfrac{3}{8}, 6\dfrac{1}{3}$

   B $7\dfrac{1}{10}, 7\dfrac{1}{5}, 6\dfrac{3}{8}, 6\dfrac{1}{3}$

   C $7\dfrac{1}{5}, 7\dfrac{1}{10}, 6\dfrac{1}{3}, 6\dfrac{3}{8}$

   D $6\dfrac{1}{3}, 6\dfrac{3}{8}, 7\dfrac{1}{5}, 7\dfrac{1}{10}$

6. Which set of numbers is ordered from least to greatest?

   A $1\dfrac{7}{8}, 1\dfrac{4}{5}, 1, \dfrac{11}{16}$

   B $1, \dfrac{11}{16}, 1\dfrac{4}{5}, 1\dfrac{7}{8}$

   C $\dfrac{11}{16}, 1, 1\dfrac{4}{5}, 1\dfrac{7}{8}$

   D $\dfrac{11}{16}, 1, 1\dfrac{7}{8}, 1\dfrac{4}{5}$

7. Ami completed a race in $12\frac{2}{5}$ seconds. Ben completed the race in $11\frac{3}{10}$ seconds. Sean completed the race in $11\frac{1}{4}$ seconds. Drew completed the race in $11\frac{5}{8}$ seconds. Who finished first in this race?

A Ami

B Ben

C Sean

D Drew

8. In the situation described in problem 7, who finished last?

A Ami

B Ben

C Sean

D Drew

9. Kyle has wrenches with openings measuring $\frac{1}{2}$ in., $\frac{1}{4}$ in., $\frac{3}{8}$ in., and $\frac{7}{16}$ in. How are these measurements ordered from least to greatest?

A $\frac{1}{2}$ in., $\frac{7}{16}$ in., $\frac{3}{8}$ in., $\frac{1}{4}$ in.

B $\frac{1}{4}$ in., $\frac{3}{8}$ in., $\frac{7}{16}$ in., $\frac{1}{2}$ in.

C $\frac{1}{2}$ in., $\frac{1}{4}$ in., $\frac{3}{8}$ in., $\frac{7}{16}$ in.

D $\frac{1}{4}$ in., $\frac{7}{16}$ in., $\frac{3}{8}$ in., $\frac{1}{2}$ in.

10. Saffron is a spice used in cooking. When you buy it in a store, it comes in very light packages, since it is rather expensive. Which of the following weights would be the lightest package of saffron?

A $\frac{1}{2}$ ounce

B $\frac{1}{4}$ ounce

C $\frac{3}{16}$ ounce

D $\frac{1}{5}$ ounce

11. How are the saffron packages in problem 10 ordered from greatest to least?

A $\frac{3}{16}, \frac{1}{5}, \frac{1}{4}, \frac{1}{2}$

B $\frac{3}{16}, \frac{1}{2}, \frac{1}{4}, \frac{1}{5}$

C $\frac{1}{2}, \frac{1}{4}, \frac{3}{16}, \frac{1}{5}$

D $\frac{1}{2}, \frac{1}{4}, \frac{1}{5}, \frac{3}{16}$

Show your work on a separate sheet of paper.

12. Pilar is responsible for the operation of a clock at an astronomical observatory. It is very important that the clock be accurate, and so Pilar must guarantee that the clock's time differs from the actual time by no more than $\frac{1}{100}$ of a second over the course of a year. This year, the measured difference was $\frac{7}{1,000}$ of a second. Does Pilar's clock meet the accuracy test? Explain your reasoning.

Show What You Know

M5N4.g.   Add and subtract common fractions and mixed numbers with unlike denominators.

Before you begin this lesson on adding and subtracting fractions and mixed numbers, answer these questions. Choose the letter of the correct answer for each problem.

1. $\frac{1}{3} + \frac{1}{3} = \square$

   What is the sum?

   A $\frac{2}{3}$

   B $\frac{1}{3}$

   C $\frac{2}{9}$

   D $\frac{1}{6}$

2. What is $\frac{5}{12} - \frac{3}{12}$?

   A $\frac{3}{4}$

   B $\frac{2}{3}$

   C $\frac{1}{4}$

   D $\frac{1}{6}$

3. $2\frac{4}{9} + 6\frac{7}{9} = \square$

   Which mixed number completes the number sentence?

   A $8\frac{1}{3}$

   B $8\frac{2}{9}$

   C $9\frac{2}{9}$

   D $9\frac{11}{9}$

4. Shawana reads $\frac{1}{3}$ of her book Monday. On Tuesday, she reads another $\frac{2}{5}$ of her book. How much of her book did she read in all on Monday and Tuesday?

   A $\frac{3}{8}$

   B $\frac{11}{15}$

   C $\frac{4}{5}$

   D $\frac{15}{15}$

5. Mrs. Wilson bought $2\frac{1}{2}$ pounds of apples and $1\frac{5}{8}$ pounds of plums. How many more pounds of apples than plums did Mrs. Wilson buy?

   A $1\frac{1}{4}$ pounds

   B $1\frac{1}{8}$ pounds

   C 1 pound

   D $\frac{7}{8}$ pound

6. Jin walks $\frac{5}{6}$ of a mile on Saturday. On Sunday, he walks $\frac{1}{3}$ of a mile less than he walked on Saturday. How far did Jin walk on Sunday?

   A $\frac{1}{4}$ mile

   B $\frac{1}{2}$ mile

   C $1\frac{1}{6}$ miles

   D $1\frac{1}{3}$ miles

LESSON
3
Adding and
Subtracting Fractions
and Mixed Numbers

Guided Instruction 1

M5N4.g.   Add and subtract common fractions and mixed numbers with unlike denominators.

When you add or subtract fractions and mixed numbers, you need to pay close attention to the denominator of the fractions. You will first study how to add and subtract fractions and mixed numbers with the same denominator.

$\frac{3}{8} + \frac{1}{8} = \boxed{}$

What is the sum?

Think About It

Add the fractions to find the sum. You can use fraction strips to show each fraction. Then, count how many to find the sum.

$$\boxed{\frac{1}{8}}\,\boxed{\frac{1}{8}}\,\boxed{\frac{1}{8}} + \boxed{\frac{1}{8}} = \boxed{\frac{1}{8}}\,\boxed{\frac{1}{8}}\,\boxed{\frac{1}{8}}\,\boxed{\frac{1}{8}}$$

$$\frac{3}{8} \quad + \quad \frac{1}{8} \quad = \quad \frac{4}{8}$$

Now write the sum in **simplest form**.

$$\boxed{\frac{1}{8}}\,\boxed{\frac{1}{8}}\,\boxed{\frac{1}{8}}\,\boxed{\frac{1}{8}}$$

$$\boxed{\qquad\frac{1}{2}\qquad}$$

$$\frac{4}{8} = \frac{1}{2}$$

So, $\frac{3}{8} + \frac{1}{8} = \frac{1}{2}$.

Try This Strategy

Add the Numerators

If two fractions have the same **denominator**, add the **numerators** to find the sum. The denominator stays the same.

What is the sum of $\frac{1}{5}$ and $\frac{2}{5}$?

$\frac{1}{5} + \frac{2}{5} = \frac{3}{5}$

You can use the same strategy for subtraction.

Study the problem. Use the **Math Guide** for tips that can help you understand how to subtract mixed numbers with the same, or like, denominators.

 Math Guide

Rewrite the problem vertically. Line up the whole numbers and fractions.	What is $6\frac{3}{4} - 2\frac{1}{4}$?
First, subtract the fractions.	$\begin{array}{r} 6\frac{3}{4} \\ -\ 2\frac{1}{4} \\ \hline \frac{2}{4} \end{array}$
Then, subtract the whole numbers.	$\begin{array}{r} \mathbf{6}\frac{3}{4} \\ -\ \mathbf{2}\frac{1}{4} \\ \hline \mathbf{4}\frac{2}{4} \end{array}$
Write the difference in simplest form.	$4\frac{2}{4} = 4\frac{1}{2}$ So, $6\frac{3}{4} - 2\frac{1}{4} = 4\frac{1}{2}$.

Now, use what you already know and what you learned to add and subtract fractions and mixed numbers with like denominators.

Answer the questions on the next page.

Practice the Skill 1

M5N4.g. Add and subtract common fractions and mixed numbers with unlike denominators.

Practice adding and subtracting fractions and mixed numbers by solving the problems below.

EXAMPLE

What is $3\frac{1}{3} + 2\frac{1}{3}$?

A $5\frac{2}{6}$

B $5\frac{2}{3}$

C $1\frac{2}{6}$

D $\frac{2}{3}$

What do you need to find?

Find the sum by adding the fractions and then the whole numbers.

$$3\frac{1}{3}$$
$$+ \ 2\frac{1}{3}$$
$$\overline{\ \ 5\frac{2}{3}}$$

Now read each question. Circle the letter of the correct answer. You may use fraction strips.

1. $\frac{9}{10} - \frac{6}{10} = \boxed{}$

What is the difference?

A $\frac{3}{20}$

B $\frac{3}{10}$

C $\frac{3}{5}$

D $\frac{3}{0}$

2. What is $\frac{1}{4} + \frac{1}{4}$?

A $\frac{2}{16}$

B $\frac{2}{8}$

C $\frac{1}{2}$

D $\frac{3}{4}$

3. $7\frac{3}{8} + 3\frac{3}{8} = \boxed{}$

What is the sum?

A $10\frac{6}{16}$

B $10\frac{3}{5}$

C $10\frac{2}{3}$

D $10\frac{3}{4}$

4. What is $8\frac{6}{9} - 5\frac{3}{9}$?

A $3\frac{1}{9}$

B $3\frac{1}{3}$

C $3\frac{6}{9}$

D $3\frac{3}{1}$

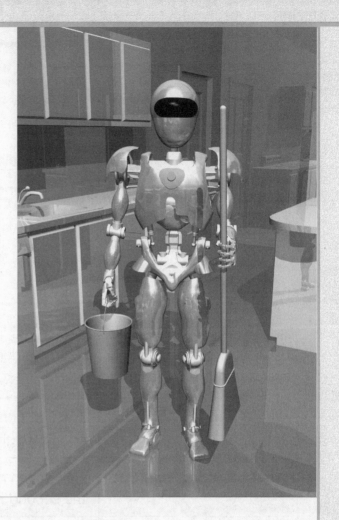

NEWS FLASH!

'Bots in the Kitchen

Pittsburgh, PA—Do you ever wish you did not have boring chores? Matt Mason feels the same way. He wants to make robots that do boring chores! He thinks these robots will give people more free time to enjoy themselves.

One type of robot will fit in a wall. The robot will blow dirt into a corner and suck it up. Then, the robot will spray cleaner on the floor. Last, it will mop up the cleaner with an arm. People would never have to mop again!

The robot could run on energy lost from the stove and oven. This would save natural resources. Imagine mopping the floor and saving resources, all without lifting a finger!

Solve It

Imagine what it would be like to have a robot help you with the chores as you answer the questions. Show your answers in simplest form. Show your work on a separate sheet of paper.

1. It takes a robot $\frac{7}{8}$ hour to clean the basement floor. The same robot takes $\frac{3}{8}$ hour to clean the bathroom floor. How much longer does it take the robot to clean the basement floor than the bathroom floor?

2. It takes one robot $1\frac{2}{5}$ hours to clean the first floor of a house. It takes the same robot $2\frac{1}{5}$ hours to clean the second floor of the house. How long does it take the robot to clean the first floor and the second floor of the house altogether?

LADDERS to SUCCESS

LESSON 3

Adding and Subtracting Fractions and Mixed Numbers

Ladder to Success

M5N4.g.   Add and subtract common fractions and mixed numbers with unlike denominators.

Review

You have learned how to add and subtract fractions and mixed numbers.

Review the methods you can use to add and subtract fractions and mixed numbers.

- You can use fraction strips.
- You can use paper and pencil.

Practice 1

Rachel weighs two bunches of grapes. The first bunch weighs $\frac{7}{8}$ pound. The second bunch weighs $\frac{5}{8}$ pound. How much more does the first bunch weigh than the second bunch?

What I Already Know	The first bunch weighs $\frac{7}{8}$ pound and the second bunch weighs $\frac{5}{8}$ pound.
What I Need to Find Out	How much more does the first bunch weigh than the second bunch?
What I Need to Do	Find $\frac{7}{8} - \frac{5}{8}$.

You can use fraction strips to solve the problem.

$\frac{1}{8}$	$\frac{1}{8}$	$\frac{1}{8}$	$\frac{1}{8}$	$\frac{1}{8}$	$\frac{1}{8}$	$\frac{1}{8}$

Cross out the fraction strips to show subtracting $\frac{5}{8}$ from $\frac{7}{8}$.

Use the models to complete the number sentence. $\frac{7}{8} - \frac{5}{8} = \boxed{}$

How much more did the first bunch weigh than the second bunch? Show your answer in simplest form. _____

1. What is $\frac{5}{9} + \frac{1}{9}$?

  A $\frac{6}{18}$

  B $\frac{1}{2}$

  C $\frac{2}{3}$

  D $\frac{3}{4}$

2. What is $\frac{3}{5} - \frac{1}{5}$?

  A $\frac{2}{0}$

  B $\frac{2}{5}$

  C $\frac{2}{10}$

  D $\frac{3}{25}$

Practice 2

At the deli, Mr. Perez buys $1\frac{1}{4}$ pounds of smoked turkey and $1\frac{3}{4}$ pounds of salami. How much smoked turkey and salami did Mr. Perez buy in all? Show your answer in simplest form.

What I Already Know	Mr. Perez bought $1\frac{1}{4}$ pounds of smoked turkey and $1\frac{3}{4}$ pounds of salami.
What I Need to Find Out	How much smoked turkey and salami did Mr. Perez buy in all?
What I Need to Do	Find $1\frac{1}{4} + 1\frac{3}{4}$.

Since $1\frac{1}{4}$ and $1\frac{3}{4}$ are mixed numbers, use paper and pencil to add the mixed numbers.

Complete the problem.

$$\begin{array}{r} 1\frac{1}{4} \\ + 1\frac{3}{4} \\ \hline \end{array}$$

When the numerator and the denominator of a fraction are the same, the fraction is equal to 1.

What is the sum in simplest form? _____

How much smoked turkey and salami did Mr. Perez buy in all? _____

---

1. $2\frac{8}{10} - 2\frac{4}{10} = \boxed{}$

What is the difference?

A $2\frac{4}{5}$

B $2\frac{2}{5}$

C $\frac{4}{5}$

D $\frac{2}{5}$

2. $\frac{5}{8} + \frac{3}{8} = \boxed{}$

What is the sum?

A 1

B $\frac{7}{8}$

C $\frac{8}{16}$

D $\frac{2}{18}$

Practice 3

Sasha is using the recipe below to make pumpkin bread.

Pumpkin Bread

2 cups pumpkin	$\frac{3}{4}$ cup oil
$1\frac{1}{2}$ cups light brown sugar	4 beaten eggs
$1\frac{1}{2}$ cups dark brown sugar	$1\frac{1}{4}$ teaspoons salt
$2\frac{3}{4}$ cups white flour	$1\frac{1}{2}$ teaspoons baking soda
$\frac{3}{4}$ cup wheat flour	1 teaspoon cinnamon

How many cups of flour are needed to make the bread? Show your answer in simplest form.

Reread the problem to see what you need to do.

You need to find out how much flour is needed to make the bread. You need to add the amount of white flour to the amount of wheat flour to find the total amount of flour. This means you should add $2\frac{3}{4}$ and $\frac{3}{4}$ to find the answer.

How can you add $2\frac{3}{4}$ and $\frac{3}{4}$?

You can add mixed numbers using paper and pencil.

Complete the addition on your own.

$$\begin{array}{r} 2\frac{3}{4} \\ +\ \ \frac{3}{4} \\ \hline \end{array}$$

Write the sum in simplest form. _____

Explain how you wrote the sum in simplest form.

_____

_____

How many cups of flour are needed to make the bread? _____

---

1. How many cups of sugar does Sasha need to make the bread? _____

2. How much more baking soda does Sasha need than salt? _____

Guided Instruction 2

M5N4.g.   Add and subtract common fractions and mixed numbers with unlike denominators.

You will build upon what you learned in Part 1 by learning to add and subtract fractions and mixed numbers with unlike denominators.

What is $\frac{3}{5} + \frac{1}{3}$?

Think About It

The fractions have different denominators, so you need to use the **least common denominator** (LCD) to solve this problem.

Find the LCD by listing the multiples of each denominator.

Multiples of 5: 5, 10, (15), 20, 25, 30

Multiples of 3: 3, 6, 9, 12, (15), 18

15 is the least common multiple of 5 and 3. Use 15 as the least common denominator.

Rename the fractions as **equivalent fractions** using the LCD.

$$\frac{3}{5} = \frac{3 \times 3}{5 \times 3} = \frac{9}{15} \qquad\qquad \frac{1}{3} = \frac{1 \times 5}{3 \times 5} = \frac{5}{15}$$

Add the equivalent fractions to find the sum.

$$\frac{9}{15} + \frac{5}{15} = \frac{14}{15}$$

So, $\frac{3}{5} + \frac{1}{3} = \frac{14}{15}$.

Try This Strategy

Denominators are Multiples

What is $\frac{3}{4} - \frac{1}{2}$?

Since 4 is a multiple of 2 and 4, only rename $\frac{1}{2}$ using 4 as the denominator.

$$\frac{1}{2} = \frac{1 \times 2}{2 \times 2} = \frac{2}{4}$$

Since $\frac{3}{4} - \frac{2}{4} = \frac{1}{4}$, then $\frac{3}{4} - \frac{1}{2} = \frac{1}{4}$.

Study the problem. Use the **Math Guide** for tips that can help you understand how to subtract mixed numbers with unlike denominators.

 Math Guide

What is $3\frac{1}{4} - 2\frac{1}{3}$?

The fractions do not have like denominators. They need to be renamed.

$$3\frac{1}{4} = 3\frac{1 \times 3}{4 \times 3} = 3\frac{3}{12}$$

$$2\frac{1}{3} = 2\frac{1 \times 4}{3 \times 4} = 2\frac{4}{12}$$

Since $\frac{3}{12} < \frac{4}{12}$, regroup $3\frac{3}{12}$ to $2\frac{15}{12}$.

$$3\frac{3}{12} = 2 + \frac{12}{12} + \frac{3}{12} = 2\frac{15}{12}$$
$$-2\frac{4}{12} = \qquad\qquad 2\frac{4}{12}$$

Subtract the fractions and then the whole numbers.

$$2\frac{15}{12}$$
$$-2\frac{4}{12}$$
$$\frac{11}{12}$$

Check that your answer is in simplest form.

So, $3\frac{1}{4} - 2\frac{1}{3} = \frac{11}{12}$.

Now, use what you already know and what you learned to add and subtract fractions and mixed numbers with unlike denominators.

Answer the questions on the next page.

LESSON

3

Adding and Subtracting Fractions and Mixed Numbers

Practice the Skill 2

M5N4.g.   Add and subtract common fractions and mixed numbers with unlike denominators.

Choose the correct answer. You may use fraction strips.

1. $\frac{3}{4} - \frac{2}{8} = \boxed{}$

    What is the difference?

    A $\frac{1}{2}$

    B $\frac{1}{4}$

    C $\frac{1}{6}$

    D $\frac{1}{8}$

2. What is $\frac{2}{3} + \frac{1}{9}$?

    A $\frac{8}{9}$

    B $\frac{7}{9}$

    C $\frac{3}{12}$

    D $\frac{1}{6}$

3. Jenna has $\frac{1}{2}$ stick of butter. She uses $\frac{1}{6}$ of the butter for a recipe. How much of the stick of butter does she have left?

    A $\frac{1}{3}$ stick

    B $\frac{1}{4}$ stick

    C $\frac{1}{12}$ stick

    D $\frac{0}{4}$ stick

4. Peter buys $2\frac{1}{2}$ pounds of strawberries and $1\frac{1}{3}$ pounds of cherries. How many pounds of fruit does Peter buy altogether?

    A $1\frac{1}{3}$ pounds

    B $3\frac{2}{5}$ pounds

    C $3\frac{5}{6}$ pounds

    D $3\frac{8}{9}$ pounds

5. $4\frac{1}{2} + 2\frac{3}{5} = \boxed{}$

    What is the sum?

    A $6\frac{1}{10}$

    B $6\frac{4}{7}$

    C $7\frac{1}{10}$

    D $7\frac{4}{7}$

6. What is $8\frac{7}{8} - 4\frac{3}{4}$?

    A $5\frac{1}{8}$

    B 5

    C $4\frac{1}{2}$

    D $4\frac{1}{8}$

AN AUTHENTIC WINTER GETAWAY

Valley Forge, PA—During the Revolutionary War, the Continental Army spent one winter in Valley Forge, Pennsylvania. Many people visit Valley Forge during the warm months, when the grass is green and it is nice outside. However, to see how the Continental Army lived, you need to visit during the winter.

When the Continental Army was at Valley Forge, the temperatures were cold and the ground was covered in slush and mud. During a summer visit, it is difficult to imagine these miserable conditions. However, during the winter you can get a better idea of what it was like for the soldiers. You can walk outdoors with the cold rain making your path slippery and your feet soaking wet. Then, you can truly imagine what life was like for the soldiers.

Solve It

Imagine two families visiting Valley Forge as you answer the questions below. Show your answers in simplest form. Show your work on a separate sheet of paper.

1. A family spends $2\frac{1}{2}$ hours at Valley Forge. They spend $1\frac{1}{4}$ hours walking around the park and the rest of the time taking an auto tour. How much time do they spend on the auto tour?

2. Another family goes to the Valley Forge Welcome Center. They first spend $\frac{2}{5}$ hour talking to the guide about the park. Then, they spend $\frac{1}{3}$ hour watching a film on Valley Forge. They then leave the Welcome Center and tour the park. How much time does the family spend at the Welcome Center in all?

Show What You Learned

M5N4.g.   Add and subtract common fractions and mixed numbers with unlike denominators.

Now that you have practiced adding and subtracting fractions and mixed numbers, take this quiz to show what you learned. Choose the letter of the correct answer for each problem.

1. $\frac{5}{6} + \frac{4}{6} = \boxed{}$

   What is the sum?

   A $1\frac{1}{2}$

   B $1\frac{1}{3}$

   C $\frac{3}{4}$

   D $\frac{1}{2}$

2. Kerry walks $\frac{5}{8}$ mile to school each day. There is a stoplight on her way to school after she walks $\frac{3}{8}$ mile. How much farther does she have to walk to get to school after she walks by the stoplight?

   A $\frac{1}{8}$ mile

   B $\frac{1}{6}$ mile

   C $\frac{1}{4}$ mile

   D $\frac{1}{3}$ of a mile

3. $5\frac{4}{7} - 2\frac{2}{7} = \boxed{}$

   Which mixed number completes the number sentence?

   A $3\frac{6}{7}$

   B $3\frac{2}{7}$

   C $2\frac{6}{7}$

   D $2\frac{2}{7}$

4. Shawn runs $9\frac{4}{5}$ miles in 1 week. He runs $2\frac{1}{3}$ miles farther the next week. How many miles did Shawn run the second week?

   A $11\frac{2}{15}$ miles

   B $11\frac{5}{8}$ miles

   C $12\frac{2}{15}$ miles

   D $12\frac{2}{3}$ miles

5. On a meat platter, there are $3\frac{3}{4}$ pounds of turkey and $2\frac{1}{2}$ pounds of ham. How much more turkey than ham is on the meat platter?

   A $1\frac{1}{2}$ pounds

   B $1\frac{1}{4}$ pounds

   C $1\frac{1}{8}$ pounds

   D $\frac{3}{4}$ pound

6. What is $\frac{5}{12} + \frac{2}{3}$?

   A $\frac{3}{4}$

   B $\frac{11}{12}$

   C $1\frac{1}{8}$

   D $1\frac{1}{12}$

7. Germaine went to lacrosse practice for $1\frac{1}{2}$ hours. He then spent $1\frac{2}{5}$ hours working on his homework. How much time did Germaine spend at lacrosse practice and working on homework?

A $2\frac{9}{10}$ hours

B $2\frac{3}{7}$ hours

C $2\frac{1}{3}$ hours

D $2\frac{2}{5}$ hours

8. A running path is $3\frac{1}{4}$ miles long. Bo has run $\frac{3}{4}$ of a mile on the path so far. How much farther does Bo have to run to complete the path?

A 4 miles

B $2\frac{3}{4}$ miles

C $2\frac{1}{2}$ miles

D $1\frac{1}{2}$ miles

9. What is $8\frac{3}{8} - 7\frac{1}{4}$?

A $1\frac{1}{8}$

B $1\frac{1}{16}$

C $\frac{1}{2}$

D $\frac{1}{8}$

10. Dalton drives $\frac{3}{4}$ mile to the bank. He then drives $3\frac{2}{3}$ miles to the grocery store. How far does Dalton drive altogether?

A $3\frac{5}{12}$ miles

B $3\frac{5}{7}$ miles

C $4\frac{5}{12}$ miles

D $4\frac{5}{7}$ miles

11. $\frac{3}{4} - \frac{5}{12} = \boxed{}$

What is the difference?

A $\frac{1}{4}$

B $\frac{1}{3}$

C $\frac{1}{2}$

D $\frac{5}{8}$

Show your work on a separate sheet of paper.

12. Explain the steps you use to find and record the sum of $\frac{3}{4}$ and $\frac{5}{12}$ in simplest form.

Show What You Know

M5N4.h.–M5N5.a.   Use fractions and decimals interchangeably; Model percent on 10 by 10 grids.

Before you begin this lesson on fractions, decimals, and percents, answer these questions. Choose the letter of the correct answer for each problem.

1. Which shows 50% written as a decimal?

   A 50.0

   B 5.0

   C 0.5

   D 0.05

2. Which grid has 60% shaded?

   A

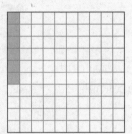

   B

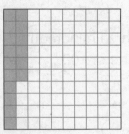

   C

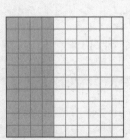

   D

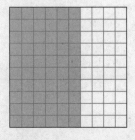

3. Which fraction represents the shaded part of the grid?

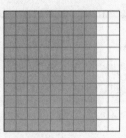

   A $\frac{2}{10}$

   B $\frac{1}{20}$

   C $\frac{2}{25}$

   D $\frac{4}{5}$

4. Which is $\frac{2}{8}$ written as a percent?

   A 25%

   B 28%

   C 40%

   D 80%

5. Which fraction is equivalent to 1%?

   A $\frac{1}{1000}$

   B $\frac{1}{100}$

   C $\frac{1}{10}$

   D $\frac{1}{1}$

LESSON
4
Connecting Fractions, Decimals, and Percents

Guided Instruction 1

M5N4.h.–M5N5.a.   Use fractions and decimals interchangeably; Model percent on 10 by 10 grids.

Fractions, decimals, and **percents** can be used to name part of a whole. In Part 1, you will study how to identify fractions, decimals, and percents using models.

Write a fraction, decimal, and percent for the shaded part of the grid.

Think About It

Count the number of shaded parts compared to the number of total parts. You can use this information to write a percent, fraction, and decimal.

The grid has 33 out of 100 squares shaded.

You can write this as a fraction: $\frac{33}{100}$

You can write this as a decimal: 0.33

> 0.33 is thirty-three hundredths or 33 parts of 100.

You can write this as a percent: 33%

> 33% means 33 parts of 100.

So, you can represent the shaded part of the grid as $\frac{33}{100}$, 0.33, or 33%.

Try This Strategy

Shade a Grid

Represent 73% on a grid.

73% means 73 parts of 100.
Shade 73 small squares on the grid to show 73%.

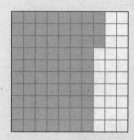

Study the problem. Use the **Math Guide** for tips that can help you understand how fractions, decimals, and percents are connected.

Math Guide	
Each square represents $\frac{1}{100}$, 0.01, or 1%.	Write a fraction, decimal, and percent for the shaded part of the grid. 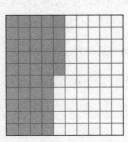
To write the fraction, show: number of shaded parts total number of parts. Then simplify.	$\frac{45}{100}$ of the grid is shaded. $\frac{45}{100} = \frac{45 \div 5}{100 \div 5} = \frac{9}{20}$
To find the decimal, think: How many hundredths are shaded?	0.45 of the grid is shaded.
To find the percent, think: How many squares out of 100 are shaded?	45% of the grid is shaded. I can represent the shaded part of the grid as $\frac{9}{20}$, 0.45, or 45%.

Now, use what you already know and what you learned to relate fractions, decimals, and percents using grids.

Answer the questions on the next page.

Practice the Skill 1

M5N4.h.–M5N5.a. Use fractions and decimals interchangeably; Model percent on 10 by 10 grids.

Practice connecting fractions, decimals, and percents by solving the problems below.

EXAMPLE

Which decimal represents the shaded part of the grid?

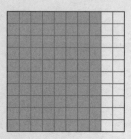

A 0.08

B 0.8

C 0.88

D 0.9

What do you need to find?

Find the decimal shown by the grid.
Count the total number of shaded parts.

80 parts of 100 are shaded.

0.80 can also be written as 0.8.

Now, read each question.
Circle the letter of the correct answer.
Use the grid for both questions.

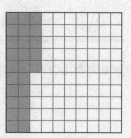

1. Which percent represents the shaded part of the grid?

    A 20%

    B 25%

    C 52%

    D 75%

2. Which fraction represents the shaded part of the grid?

    A $\frac{3}{4}$

    B $\frac{1}{3}$

    C $\frac{1}{4}$

    D $\frac{1}{25}$

RETURN TO SENDER

Wilmington, DE—Angie Turochy got a returned letter in the mail. She thought the letter went to the wrong address. Inside she found a letter that was lost for over 50 years!

Turochy works for the Chamber of Commerce in Delaware. She was surprised to get a letter back that was about visiting the state in the 1950s. She wondered why the letter was returned after such a long time. She learned that the post office tries to deliver lost letters. Sometimes they cannot deliver a letter. When that happens, the letter is returned to the sender.

No one knows how the letter was lost. But people are glad the letter was found. It shows a little bit of what Delaware was like in the 1950s.

Solve It

Think about the letters the post offices loses and finds each year as you answer each question below.

1. The grid shows what percent of mail one post office loses each year. Write this number as a percent.

_____

2. Another post office finds 98% of all mail that was identified as lost. Shade the grid to show this percent.

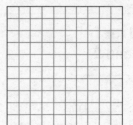

Ladder to Success

M5N4.h.–M5N5.a.   Use fractions and decimals interchangeably; Model percent on 10 by 10 grids.

Review

You have learned how to connect fractions, decimals, and percents using grids.

Review the steps you can use to connect fractions, decimals, and percents.

- You can write a fraction, decimal, or percent to represent the shaded part of a grid.
- You can shade a grid to represent a fraction, decimal, or percent.

Practice 1

Coach Ray wants to shade a grid to show the percentage of games the soccer team won during their season. They won 57% of their games. How can Coach Ray shade the grid to show the percentage of wins?

What I Already Know	The soccer team won 57% of their games.
What I Need to Find Out	How can Coach Ray show the percent of wins on a grid?
What I Need to Do	Shade the grid to show 57%.

Complete the statement below.

57% means ☐ parts of 100.

Shade the grid to show 57%.

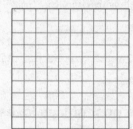

How can Coach Ray show the percentage of wins as a decimal? _____

How can Coach Ray show the percentage of wins as a fraction? _____

Use the grid for problems 1 and 2.

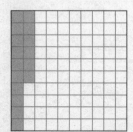

1. Which fraction represents the shaded part of the grid?

   A $\frac{16}{10}$

   B $\frac{4}{25}$

   C $\frac{3}{5}$

   D $\frac{7}{8}$

2. Which decimal represents the shaded part of the grid?

   A 0.16

   B 0.26

   C 0.61

   D 0.84

Practice 2

Madison surveyed 100 people to find out if they liked going to the movies. She made a grid and shaded a square for each person who said that they like to go to the movies.

How can Madison represent as a percent, a fraction, and a decimal the number of people who said that they like to go to the movies?

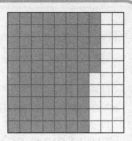

What I Already Know	Madison surveyed 100 people. The shaded part of the grid shows the people who like to go to the movies.
What I Need to Find Out	How can Madison show the results of the survey as a percent, fraction, and decimal?
What I Need to Do	Use the grid to solve the problem.

Use the shaded grid to complete the statements below.

The grid has ☐ out of 100 squares shaded.

Percent: ☐ parts of 100 = ☐ %

Fraction: $\dfrac{☐}{100} = \dfrac{☐}{☐}$

Decimal: seventy-five hundredths = 0.☐

Madison can show the percentage of people who like to go to the movies as

_____, _____, or _____.

Use the grid for problems 1 and 2.

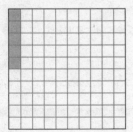

1. Which percent represents the shaded part of the grid?

   A 0.5%   C 15.0%

   B 5.0%   D 50.0%

2. Which fraction represents the shaded part of the grid?

   A $\frac{2}{5}$ C $\frac{1}{25}$

   B $\frac{1}{5}$ D $\frac{1}{20}$

Practice 3

The Ice Cream Shack sold ice cream cones. On Saturday, exactly $\frac{1}{2}$ of their sales were for vanilla ice cream cones.

Shade the grid to show the fraction that represents the sales of vanilla ice cream cones as a part of their total sales.

Reread the problem to see what you need to do.

You need to shade the grid to show $\frac{1}{2}$.

How can you shade the grid to show $\frac{1}{2}$?

Rewrite the fraction, so it has a denominator of 100.

$$\frac{1}{2} = \frac{\boxed{} \times 50}{\boxed{} \times 50} = \frac{\boxed{}}{\boxed{}}$$

Shade the grid to show $\boxed{}$ out of 100 parts are shaded.

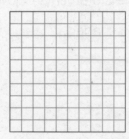

Now, use the shaded grid to answer the questions.

1. What percent of the total sales were for vanilla ice cream cones?

_____

2. What decimal represents the sales for vanilla ice cream cones as a part of the total sales?

_____

Guided Instruction 2

M5N4.h.–M5N5.a. Use fractions and decimals interchangeably; Model percent on 10 by 10 grids.

You will build upon what you learned in Part 1 by learning to connect fractions, decimals, and percents without using a 10-by-10 grid.

Here's How

Write 0.85 as a percent.

Think About It

Decimals and percents are related, so you can **convert** the decimal to a percent.

Write the decimal as a fraction with 100 as the denominator.

$0.85 = \frac{85}{100}$ Think: 0.85 is eighty-five hundredths.

Then, write the fraction as a percent.

$\frac{85}{100} = 85\%$

So, 0.85 written as a percent is 85%.

If you want to write a percent as a decimal, simply divide the number before the percent symbol by 100. So, $62\% = \frac{62}{100} = 0.62$.

Try This Strategy

Write a Percent as a Fraction
Write 15% as a fraction.

Step 1	**Step 2**
Write the percent as a fraction with 100 as the denominator.	Simplify the fraction.
$15\% = \frac{15}{100}$	$\frac{15}{100} = \frac{3}{20}$
	$15\% = \frac{3}{20}$

Study the problem. Use the Math Guide for tips that can help you understand how to convert a fraction to a decimal and a percent.

 Math Guide

Write $\frac{1}{8}$ as a decimal and as a percent.

First, write $\frac{1}{8}$ as a decimal.	$\frac{1}{8} = 0.125$
Convert a fraction to a decimal by dividing.	
To convert the decimal to a percent, move the decimal point 2 places to the right.	0.12.5
Insert the percent symbol at the end of the number.	12.5%
	So, $\frac{1}{8} = 0.125 = 12.5\%$.

Now, use what you already know and what you learned to relate percents, fractions, and decimals.

Answer the questions on the next page.

LESSON

4

Connecting Fractions, Decimals, and Percents

Practice the Skill 2

M5N4.h.–M5N5.a. Use fractions and decimals interchangeably; Model percent on 10 by 10 grids.

Choose the correct answer.

1. Which is equivalent to $\frac{3}{8}$?

   A 37.5%

   B 37.5

   C 38.0%

   D 38.0

2. Which is 42% written as a decimal?

   A 0.042

   B 0.42

   C 4.2

   D 42.0

3. A baseball team wins $\frac{4}{5}$ of its home games. Which is the number written as a percent?

   A 20%

   B 45%

   C 60%

   D 80%

4. Tyson uses 18% of his savings to buy a CD. Which fraction is equivalent to 18%?

   A $\frac{10}{18}$

   B $\frac{1}{6}$

   C $\frac{9}{50}$

   D $\frac{1}{5}$

5. One brand of juice contains 0.05 of natural juice. Which is this decimal written as a percent?

   A 0.05%

   B 0.5%

   C 5%

   D 50%

6. Which statement is true?

   A $12\% = 0.12 = \frac{3}{25}$

   B $12\% = 0.12 = \frac{1}{12}$

   C $12\% = 1.20 = \frac{3}{25}$

   D $12\% = 1.20 = \frac{1}{12}$

A BIG SPLASH

Queensbury, NY—This winter, many families plan to spend their winter days racing down water slides, splashing in wave pools, and floating on river rides. But, families will not be heading south—they will be heading north.

Indoor water parks are a new trend in resorts. Cities in the northeast are the perfect location. These parks have water slides, wave pools, river rides, regular pools, and hot tubs the whole family can enjoy. Plus, there are arcades and laser tag games to enjoy after a day of swimming.

The water and air temperature is kept around 84°F. The indoor water parks are often attached to a hotel and restaurant. This means families never have to step into the cold air!

Solve It

Imagine you are visiting an indoor water park as you answer each question. Show your work on a separate sheet of paper.

1. By 8 o'clock in the morning, the water park has $\frac{3}{5}$ of its attractions open. What percent of attractions are open by 8 o'clock in the morning?

_____

2. The maximum number of people allowed on the Lazy River ride is 100. There are currently 70 people on the ride. How can you show this number as a percent, fraction, and decimal? Show the fraction in simplest form.

_____

_____

Show What You Learned

M5N4.h.–M5N5.a. Use fractions and decimals interchangeably; Model percent on 10 by 10 grids.

Now that you have practiced writing and relating fractions, decimals, and percents, take this quiz to show what you learned. Choose the letter of the correct answer for each problem.

1. Horatio shades a grid to show $\frac{3}{4}$. Which grid did he shade?

A

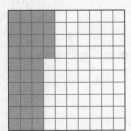

B

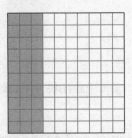

C

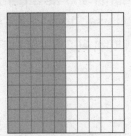

D

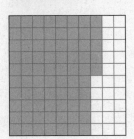

2. Which shows 3% written as a decimal?

A 0.003

B 0.03

C 0.3

D 3.0

3. The Bulldogs win 0.64 of their games. Which shows the Bulldogs' wins written as a percent?

A 0.64%

B 6.4%

C 64%

D 640%

4. Which is $\frac{5}{8}$ written as a decimal?

A 0.625

B 6.25

C 62.5

D 625.0

5. The Golden Crust Bakery sold 88% of the bread in the store. Which shows the bread sales written as a fraction?

A $\frac{7}{8}$

B $\frac{22}{25}$

C $\frac{3}{4}$

D $\frac{8}{75}$

6. Which statement is true?

A $\frac{3}{20} = 0.20 = 20\%$

B $\frac{3}{20} = 0.15 = 1.5\%$

C $\frac{3}{20} = 0.15 = 15\%$

D $\frac{3}{20} = 2.00 = 2.0\%$

7. Ginger studied her spelling words for $\frac{1}{4}$ hour. For what percent of an hour did Ginger study her spelling words?

A 14%

B 25%

C 40%

D 75%

8. Which decimal is equivalent to 50%?

A 0.50

B 0.20

C 0.05

D 0.02

9. A quarterback completes 65% of his passes in one game. Which is this percent written as a fraction in simplest form?

A $\frac{65}{10}$

B $\frac{6}{5}$

C $\frac{13}{25}$

D $\frac{13}{20}$

10. Taylor finishes $\frac{3}{5}$ of his chores before he leaves for school. He needs to finish the rest of his chores after school. What percent represents the chores Taylor needs to finish after school?

A 20%

B 40%

C 60%

D 80%

11. Which is $\frac{1}{5}$ written as a decimal?

A 0.02

B 0.05

C 0.15

D 0.20

Show your work on a separate sheet of paper.

12. Write $\frac{3}{5}$ as a decimal and as a percent. Explain the steps used to convert a fraction to a decimal and a fraction to a percent.

Show What You Know

M5P1.b.   Solve single and multi-step routine word problems related to all appropriate fifth grade math standards.

**Before you begin this lesson on word problems, answer these questions.
Choose the letter of the correct answer for each problem.**

1. Jerry measured four insects. His measurements are shown in the table below.

Which insect is the shortest?

A Insect A

B Insect B

C Insect C

D Insect D

Insect	Length (in cm)
Insect A	0.25
Insect B	0.5
Insect C	0.52
Insect D	0.2

2. Three hundred eighty-four students and adults are going on a field trip to the Bloomfield Zoo. Each bus can hold 36 people. How many buses are needed for the field trip?

A 9 buses

B 10 buses

C 11 buses

D 12 buses

3. There are 20 students in this year's school musical. Six of the students were in last year's musical. Ten students in this year's musical are also in the school band. Which percent represents the number of students that were in last year's musical and this year's musical?

A 30%

B 45%

C 50%

D 60%

4. Marco bought a movie ticket for $9.50 and a small popcorn for $3.25. He has $5.25 left over. How much money did he have to start with?

A $20.00

B $18.00

C $12.75

D $7.50

5. Robin spends $78 on a helmet and knee pads. The helmet costs $4 more than the knee pads. How much does the helmet cost?

A $37

B $39

C $41

D $43

6. Peter plants a bean plant and records its height each week. At the end of the first week, the plant is 1.8 cm tall. At the end of the second week, the plant is 2.4 cm tall. At the end of the third week, the plant is 3.0 cm tall. At the end of the fourth week, the plant is 3.6 cm tall. If the plant continues to grow at this rate, how tall will it be at the end of the sixth week?

A 4.2 cm

B 4.8 cm

C 5.4 cm

D 9.6 cm

LADDERS to SUCCESS

LESSON
5
Word Problems

Guided Instruction 1

M5P1.b.   Solve single and multi-step routine word problems related to all appropriate fifth grade math standards.

It is important to follow a process, or plan, when you solve word problems. In Part 1, you will learn how to apply a four-step problem solving process.

Which snowboarder had the highest half pipe score at the 2006 Winter Olympics?

2006 Winter Olympics Men's Snowboarding Half Pipe Scores

Name	Shaun White	Mason Aguirre	Markku Koski	Daniel Kass
Total Score	46.8	40.3	41.5	44.0

Think About It

Use the four-step problem solving process.

READ Carefully read the problem. Identify important information.
I need to find the snowboarder with the highest score.

PLAN Make a plan for solving the problem. I can compare the decimals in the table.

DO Follow your plan. Solve the problem. $46.8 > 44.0 > 41.5 > 40.3$
46.8 is the greatest decimal.

CHECK Think of another way to check your answer.
I could locate the scores on a number line and compare them.

Shaun White had the highest half pipe score in the 2006 Winter Olympics.

Try This Strategy

Use a Pattern

Bobbi uses 2 blocks for her first tower, 4 blocks for her second tower, 8 blocks for her third tower, and 16 blocks for her fourth tower. If this pattern continues, how many blocks will she use in her sixth tower?

Use a **pattern** to solve the problem. Each number in the pattern is twice the previous number.

2, 4, 8, 16, 32, 64

Bobbi will use 64 blocks for her sixth tower.

Study the problem. Use the Math Guide for tips that can help you understand how to choose an operation to solve a word problem.

 Math Guide

The school library has 1,318 fiction books and 2,093 nonfiction books. How many books does the school library have in all?

Read carefully to identify the question you need to answer.

READ
What do you need to find out?
You need to find out how many books are in the school library.

What important information is in the problem?
There are 1,318 fiction books and 2,093 nonfiction books.

Key words can help choose the operation. But understanding the word problem is the **best** way to choose the operation.

PLAN
Which operation can you use to solve this problem?

addition	used to join two or more groups
subtraction	used to separate a part from a whole or compare groups
multiplication	used to find out how many are in equal groups
division	used to find how many groups or how many in each group

Since you are joining two groups, use addition.

Complete the operations carefully.

DO

$$\begin{array}{r} 1,318 \\ + 2,093 \\ \hline 3,411 \end{array}$$

You can use subtraction to check addition because they are **inverse operations**.

CHECK

$$\begin{array}{r} 1,318 \\ + 2,093 \\ \hline 3,411 \end{array} \qquad \begin{array}{r} 3,411 \\ - 2,093 \\ \hline 1,318 \end{array}$$

Now, use what you already know and what you learned to solve word problems.

Answer the questions on the next page.

Practice the Skill 1

M5P1.b.   Solve single and multi-step routine word problems related to all appropriate fifth grade math standards.

Practice using the four-step process by solving the problems below.

EXAMPLE

Mr. O'Reilly bought 7 copies of a new computer game for the school computer lab. Each copy of the game cost $49.49. How much did Mr. O'Reilly spend in all?

A $7.07

B $283.86

C $243.00

D $346.43

READ What do you need to find?

Find the total amount that Mr. O'Reilly spent in all for the computer games.

PLAN How will you solve the problem?

Use multiplication.

DO
$$\begin{array}{r} \$49.49 \\ \times \quad 7 \\ \hline \$346.43 \end{array}$$

CHECK $346.43 \div 7 = \$49.49$

Now, read each question. Circle the letter of the correct answer.

1. Tori made bracelets for the school fair. She had 1,058 beads and used them all to make 23 bracelets. Each bracelet has the same number of beads. How many beads are on each bracelet?

   A 23 beads

   B 41 beads

   C 46 beads

   D 53 beads

2. Pat cuts ribbon for a design he is making. His first piece of ribbon is 4 inches long. The next piece of ribbon is $3\frac{3}{4}$ inches long. The third piece of ribbon is $3\frac{1}{2}$ inches long. The fourth piece of ribbon is $3\frac{1}{4}$ inches long. If Pat continues this pattern, how long will the seventh piece of ribbon be?

   A $2\frac{1}{4}$ in.

   B $2\frac{1}{2}$ in.

   C $2\frac{3}{4}$ in.

   D 3 in.

Name That Planet

Paris, France—Discovering a new planet does not mean that you can name it anything you want. You need to follow a set of rules.

Planet Naming Rules:

- name must be 16 letters or less
- name must be one word
- no brand names
- political names can only be used after 100 years after the person's death
- name must be different from planet names already used

Some planet names that are now used are Sabine, Lupo, von Matt, and Zeus. If you hope to find a new planet, you might want to think about its name now!

Solve It

Imagine that you are on the team that decides if a planet name can be used. Show your work on a separate sheet of paper.

1. A scientist wants to name a planet that she discovered *Persephone*. Could the name be used? Explain why or why not.

_____

_____

2. Another scientist wants to name a planet *Eisenhower*. President Eisenhower died in 1969. What will be the first year a planet can be named after President Eisenhower?

_____

Ladder to Success

M5P1.b.   Solve single and multi-step routine word problems related to all appropriate fifth grade math standards.

Review

You have learned how to use the four-step process to solve word problems.

Review the steps you can use to solve word problems.

- Follow the four-step process to read, plan, do, and check.
- Use patterns and choose the operation to solve problems.

Practice 1

The soccer league has a barbecue for the players. There are 137 players in the soccer league. Each table seats 12 people. How many tables are needed for the barbecue?

READ What I Already Know	There are 137 players in the soccer league. Each table seats 12 people.
PLAN What I Need to Find Out What I Need to Do	How many tables are needed for the barbecue? Use division to solve the problem.
DO	Complete the division problem. $12\overline{)137}$
CHECK	Show how to check your work.

The answer shows there are _____ full tables and _____ people left over.

You need to add 1 to the quotient, so there are enough seats for everyone.

How many tables are needed for the barbecue? _____

---

1. Coach Green stores the soccer balls in large bags. Each bag holds 9 soccer balls. How many bags are needed to store 78 soccer balls?

   A 8 bags   C 10 bags
   B 9 bags   D 11 bags

2. Tickets to a soccer game are $15 each. Paulo has $52. What is the greatest number of tickets Paulo can buy?

   A 5 tickets   C 3 tickets
   B 4 tickets   D 2 tickets

Practice 2

It takes John 33 minutes to ride his bike from his house to the grocery store. John arrives at the grocery store at 3:10 P.M. What time did he leave his house?

READ What I Already Know	John got to the store at 3:10 P.M. The ride took him 33 minutes.
PLAN What I Need to Find Out What I Need to Do	What time did John leave his house? I can work backward to solve the problem.
DO Work Backward	End time: 3:10 P.M. Elapsed time: [:] minutes → Time to ride to the grocery store. Start time: [:] P.M.
CHECK Work Forward	Start time: [:] P.M. Elapsed time: [:] minutes End time: [:] P.M.

What time did John leave his house? _____

1. Mrs. Goswami bought peaches for $1.45 and apples for $2.30 at the farmer's market. She had $3.25 left after her purchases. How much money did Mrs. Goswami have when she went to the farmer's market?

   A $7.00
   B $5.55
   C $3.75
   D $0.85

2. Yuri wants to eat lunch 55 minutes before he goes to soccer practice. If soccer practice starts at 1:30 P.M., what time should Yuri eat his lunch?

   A 2:45 P.M.
   B 1:15 P.M.
   C 12:55 P.M.
   D 12:35 P.M.

Practice 3

Brad is helping his parents put up a fence around their pool. The fence is 32 feet long, 24 feet wide, and will have a fence post every 4 feet. How many fence posts do they need?

Reread the problem to see what you need to do.

You need to solve the problem to find out how many fence posts are needed to build the fence.

How can you determine the number of fence posts?

You could try to solve the problem using multiplication and addition, but this problem is a little tricky. You need to think about what will happen at the corners of the fence. Another way to solve this problem is to draw a diagram.

Examine the fence posts placed on one side of the diagram below.

Complete the diagram by drawing fence posts on the other three sides of the diagram.

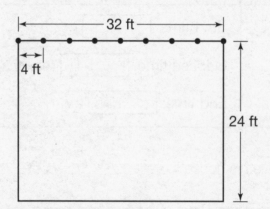

How many fence posts are needed for the entire fence?

_____

How do you know your answer is reasonable?

_____

_____

Guided Instruction 2

M5P1.b.   Solve single and multi-step routine word problems related to all appropriate fifth grade math standards.

Introduction

You will build upon what you learned in Part 1 by learning to solve more difficult word problems, including problems with extra information and multistep problems.

Here's How

There are 15 students in the ski club. Three of those students are also on the student council. Five of the students in the ski club are also in the school chorus. What percent represents the number of students that are in the ski club and on the student council?

Think About It

Use the four-step problem solving process.

READ Identify important information. Identify any extra information. *Important* information: Fifteen students are in the ski club; 3 of those students are on the student council. *Extra* information: Five of those students are in the school chorus.

PLAN Make a plan for solving the problem.
I can write a fraction and convert it to a percent.

DO Follow your plan. Solve the problem. $\frac{3}{15} = 0.20 = 20\%$

CHECK How can you tell if your answer is reasonable? I can use my understanding of percents and fractions to know that 20% is a reasonable answer.

So, 20% of students are in the ski club and on the student council.

Try This Strategy

Guess and Check

Andy has 6 pets. Some of the pets are dogs. Some of the pets are birds. Andy's pets have 20 legs in all. How many dogs does Andy have? How many birds does Andy have?

Guess and check to solve this problem.

Guess: 5 dogs, 1 bird
Check: $(5 \times 4) + (1 \times 2) = 22$
22 > 20, try a smaller number of dogs

Guess: 4 dogs, 2 birds
Check: $(4 \times 4) + (2 \times 2) = 20$
Andy has 4 dogs and 2 birds.

Study the problem. Use the Math Guide for tips that can help you understand how to solve a multistep word problem.

 Math Guide

Morin's Sports Shop offers scuba diving classes 8 times each month. The maximum number of students per class is 15. So far, $\frac{4}{5}$ of the class spaces for June are filled. How many students have signed up for classes in June?

Read carefully to understand the problem.

READ

What do you need to find out? You need to find out how many students have signed up for classes in June.

This is a multistep problem.

What important information is in the problem? There are 8 scuba classes each month; 15 students can attend each class; and $\frac{4}{5}$ of the spaces are filled for June.

Decide how to solve each step, and in what order.

PLAN

Which operations can you use to solve this problem?

First, you need to multiply to find out how many students can attend classes each month. Then, you need to find $\frac{4}{5}$ of that number.

Complete the operations carefully.

DO

$15 \times 8 = 120$

$120 \times \frac{4}{5} = 96$

Use the steps in a different order to check your work.

CHECK

$15 \times \frac{4}{5} = 12$

$12 \times 8 = 96$

So, 96 students are signed up for scuba classes in June.

Now, use what you already know and what you learned to solve word problems.

Answer the questions on the next page.

Practice the Skill 2

M5P1.b.   Solve single and multi-step routine word problems related to all appropriate fifth grade math standards.

Choose the correct answer.

1. Teddy has 63 books on 2 bookshelves. On the longer bookshelf, he has 5 more books than on the shorter bookshelf. How many books does Teddy have on the shorter bookshelf?

   A 25 books
   B 28 books
   C 29 books
   D 33 books

2. Charlie and Tag rented bikes for $22.50 per hour each. How much will it cost Charlie and Tag to rent both bikes for 5 hours?

   A $100.50
   B $112.50
   C $125.50
   D $225.00

3. Caroline collected 45 flowers from the garden. One-fifth of the flowers were tulips and $\frac{1}{9}$ of the flowers were sunflowers. How many of the flowers were tulips?

   A 5 flowers
   B 9 flowers
   C 15 flowers
   D 19 flowers

4. Pan spends $60 on a backpack and hiking boots. The hiking boots cost $6 more than the backpack. How much do the hiking boots cost?

   A $24
   B $26
   C $33
   D $36

5. Twenty-eight students are signed up for the cross country team. Seven of those students are also on the volleyball team. Fourteen students on the cross country team are also on the soccer team. What percent of the students on the cross country team are also on the volleyball team?

   A 25%   C 35%
   B 31%   D 50%

6. Which shows the correct order of operations used to solve the problem below?

   > There are 18 students in the school band. One-sixth of those students play flute. Two of the students who play flute are going to a statewide competition. How many students who play flute are not going to the statewide competition?

   A Multiply and then subtract.
   B Subtract and then multiply.
   C Divide and then subtract.
   D Subtract and then divide.

Extreme Testing

Iqaluit, Canada—Before being put into service, the Airbus A380 will fly from France to Canada for extreme cold-weather testing. The Airbus A380 has a 2-story cabin that can hold 555 passengers on trips up to 8,700 miles long.

The designers want to be sure that the jumbo jet can perform well in extreme weather. So, they will store and fly the plane in and around Iqaluit, Canada where the conditions can be as cold as −40°C. After this round of tests is complete, the jet will then be flown closer to the equator, where the jet can be tested in extremely hot conditions.

After the extreme testing is completed, the Airbus A380 will be ready for passenger flights. There are already 159 orders for the jumbo jets from clients all over the world.

Solve It

Answer each question. Show your work on a separate sheet of paper.

1. Of the 555 seats on the Airbus A380, 118 of the seats are first-class. The remaining seats are coach-class seats. How many coach-class seats are on the Airbus A380?

2. The flight from Paris to New Delhi is 5,679 miles. What is the difference between the maximum distance the Airbus A380 can fly and the distance of the flight from Paris to New Delhi?

Show What You Learned

M5P1.b.   Solve single and multi-step routine word problems related to all appropriate fifth grade math standards.

Now that you have practiced solving word problems, take this quiz to show what you learned. Choose the letter of the correct answer for each problem.

1. Mr. Pang is building a rectangular dog run using fence. The dog run is 3 meters wide and 5 meters long. He uses a fence post every 0.5 meter. How many fence posts does he need for the run?

   A 36 fence posts

   B 33 fence posts

   C 32 fence posts

   D 30 fence posts

2. One hundred seventy-five people are going on a bus trip to an amusement park. Each bus can hold 26 people. How many buses are needed for all of the passengers?

   A 5 buses

   B 6 buses

   C 7 buses

   D 8 buses

3. Hans measured the density of 4 liquids. His measurements are shown in the table below. Which liquid has the highest density?

Liquid	Density (in grams per milliliter)
Liquid A	1.25
Liquid B	1.5
Liquid C	1.0
Liquid D	0.75

   A Liquid A

   B Liquid B

   C Liquid C

   D Liquid D

4. Lourdes bought a DVD for $19.99 and a book for $14.95. She has $10.56 left over. How much money did she have to start with?

   A $45.50

   B $44.90

   C $34.94

   D $19.34

5. Connie arranges her photos in her scrapbook. Her scrapbook has 49 pages. She places 4 photos on each of 7 pages and 3 photos on each remaining page. How many photos are in her scrapbook?

   A 28 photos

   B 126 photos

   C 149 photos

   D 154 photos

6. Ben arranges his books on 4 shelves in his room. Three of the shelves have 15 books on them. The other shelf has 12 books on it. How many books does Ben have on his shelves?

   A 57 books

   B 60 books

   C 72 books

   D 75 books

7. The entertainment store had a sale on used DVDs. Any new movie DVD was on sale for $7.79. Any children's movie DVD was on sale for $4.49. Kate bought 3 new movie DVDs at the sale. How much did she spend altogether?

   A $27.86

   B $23.37

   C $21.26

   D $13.47

8. Danny made towers for a castle using 648 blocks. His castle had 4 towers. Each tower was made from the same number of blocks. How many blocks were used to build each tower?

   A 112 blocks

   B 152 blocks

   C 162 blocks

   D 192 blocks

9. Which shows the correct order of operations used to solve the problem below?

   > There are 30 children in the community swimming pool. One-fifth of those children are wearing goggles. Four of the children who are wearing goggles are also wearing swim caps. How many children are wearing goggles but not wearing swim caps?

   A Add and then multiply.

   B Add and then subtract.

   C Multiply and then subtract.

   D Multiply and then add.

10. Veronica wants to get to school 45 minutes before classes start, so she can go to the library. If classes start at 8:10 A.M., what time should Veronica arrive at school?

    A 7:25 A.M.

    B 7:35 A.M.

    C 8:25 A.M.

    D 8:55 A.M.

11. Tickets to the community theater play are $17 each. Miss Prince has $82. What is the greatest number of tickets she can buy?

    A 3 tickets

    B 4 tickets

    C 5 tickets

    D 6 tickets

Show your work on a separate sheet of paper.

12. Read the problem below. Describe the strategy you will use to solve the problem. Then, solve the problem using that strategy.

    Aidan records the growth of a seedling in his notebook for science class. His measurements for the first 4 weeks are 2.3 cm, 2.7 cm, 3.1 cm, and 3.5 cm. If the seedling continues to grow at this rate, how tall will it be in the sixth week?

Show What You Know

**Before you begin this lesson on converting measurements, answer these questions.
Choose the letter of the correct answer for each problem.**

1. 4 ft = ☐ in.

   Which number makes the sentence
   above true?

   A 16

   B 20

   C 40

   D 48

2. A punch recipe calls for 2 quarts of
   cranberry juice. Marsha only has a
   1-cup measuring cup. How many cups
   of cranberry juice will Marsha need for
   the recipe?

   A 2 cups

   B 4 cups

   C 8 cups

   D 16 cups

3. 32 oz ☐ 2 lb

   Which symbol makes the statement
   above true?

   A =

   B >

   C <

   D +

4. The packaging on a juice container says
   it contains 2,000 milliliters. How many
   liters of juice does the container hold?

   A 2 liters

   B 4 liters

   C 10 liters

   D 20 liters

5. 8.2 kg = ☐ g

   Which number makes the sentence
   above true?

   A 82

   B 820

   C 8,200

   D 82,000

6. A pencil is 10 cm long. How many mm
   long is the pencil?

   A 0.01 mm

   B 0.1 mm

   C 1 mm

   D 100 mm

Guided Instruction 1

M5N3.b.   Compare one unit to another within a single system of measurement (e.g., 1 quart = 2 pints).

Introduction

When you **convert** measurements, you need to know equivalent measures. In Part 1, you will learn how to convert **customary units** of measure.

Here's How

How many feet are equal to 84 inches?

Think About It

Use a conversion table to help you convert inches to feet.

The table shows that 1 foot = 12 inches.

Divide to convert from a smaller unit (inches) to a larger unit (feet).

84 inches = ? feet

84 ÷ 12 = 7

So, 84 inches = 7 feet.

Customary Units of **Length**
1 foot (ft) = 12 inches (in.)
1 yard (yd) = 36 in.
1 yd = 3 ft
1 mile (mi) = 5,280 ft
1 mi = 1,760 yd

Try This Strategy

Use Multiplication to Convert Measures

How many ounces are in 3 pounds?

The table shows that 1 pound = 16 ounces.

Multiply to convert from a larger unit (pounds) to a smaller unit (ounces).

3 pounds = ? ounces

3 × 16 = 48

So, 3 pounds = 48 ounces.

Customary Units of **Weight**
1 pound (lb) = 16 ounces (oz)
1 ton (T) = 2,000 lb

Study the problem. Use the Math Guide for tips that can help you understand how to convert customary units of capacity.

📐 **Math Guide**	24 pints = ☐ gallons What number completes the statement above?

<table>
<tr><th colspan="2">Customary Units of Capacity</th></tr>
<tr><td colspan="2">1 cup (c) = 8 fluid ounces (fl oz)</td></tr>
<tr><td colspan="2">1 pint (pt) = 2 c</td></tr>
<tr><td colspan="2">1 quart (qt) = 2 pt</td></tr>
<tr><td colspan="2">1 gallon (gal) = 4 qt</td></tr>
</table>

The table does not show how to convert pints directly to gallons. This is a *two-step* problem.

Use 1 quart = 2 pints for your conversion.

First, change pints to quarts.

24 pints = ? quarts

$24 \div 2 = 12$

24 pints = 12 quarts

Use 1 gallon = 4 quarts for your conversion.

Next, change quarts to gallons.

12 quarts = ? gallons

$12 \div 4 = 3$

12 quarts = 3 gallons

Check that your answer is reasonable.

So, 24 pints = 3 gallons.

Now, use what you already know and what you learned to convert customary measurements.

Answer the questions on the next page.

Practice the Skill 1

M5N3.b.   Compare one unit to another within a single system of measurement (e.g., 1 quart = 2 pints).

Practice converting customary measurements by solving the problems below.

EXAMPLE

78 in. = ☐ ft.

Which number completes the statement above?

A 6 ft

B $6\frac{1}{2}$ ft

C 7 ft

D $7\frac{4}{5}$ ft

What do you need to find?

Find how many feet are equal to 78 inches.
Use division to convert inches to feet.

$$\begin{array}{r} 6R6 \\ 12\overline{)78} \\ -72 \\ \hline 6 \end{array}$$

Show the remainder as a fraction and simplify.

$$6\frac{6}{12} = 6\frac{1}{2}$$

So, 78 in. = $6\frac{1}{2}$ ft

Now, read each question. Circle the letter of the correct answer.

1. How many pounds are in 2.5 tons?

    A   250 pounds

    B   500 pounds

    C   2,500 pounds

    D   5,000 pounds

2. 16 fluid ounces = ☐ cups

    Which number makes the sentence above true?

    A 1

    B 2

    C 3

    D 4

ANCIENT SEA MONSTERS

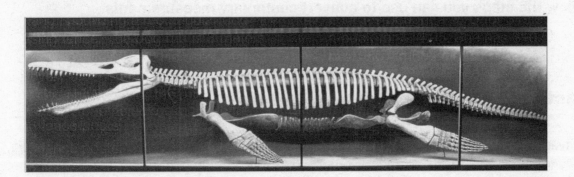

Scotland—Many people have heard stories about sea monsters. One of the most famous is the Loch Ness monster, Nessie. People describe Nessie as looking like a very large reptile. No one has proved Nessie exists or existed, but fossils show that very large reptiles used to live in the seas.

The *Kronosaurus* was a giant reptile. These animals lived in the sea about 110 million years ago. These animals had skulls that were 7 feet long. Their teeth were the size of bananas!

Each of these animals was about 33 feet long and weighed 11 tons. They were dangerous predators.

The stories about sea monsters are linked to these fossils. People wonder if deep in the water, large sea animals still swim.

Solve It
Answer each question. Show your work on a separate sheet of paper.

1. About how many inches long was the *Kronosaurus*?

   _____

2. About how many pounds did the *Kronosaurus* weigh?

   _____

3. About how many inches long was the *Kronosaurus'* skull?

   _____

Ladder to Success

M5N3.b.   Compare one unit to another within a single system of measurement (e.g., 1 quart = 2 pints).

Review

You have learned how to convert customary units of measure.

Review the steps you can use to convert customary measurements.

- Use a conversion table to find equivalent measures.
- Use multiplication or division to convert between customary units of measure.

Practice 1

Ryan is building a picnic table. He wants the table to be $2\frac{1}{2}$ yards long. To buy lumber, Ryan needs to convert his measurement to feet. How many feet long will the picnic table be?

What I Already Know	The table will be $2\frac{1}{2}$ yards long. The measurement needs to be in feet.
What I Need to Find Out	How many feet are in $2\frac{1}{2}$ yards?
What I Need to Do	Convert $2\frac{1}{2}$ yards to feet.

Since feet are smaller than yards, use multiplication to convert the measurement.

Complete the problem below.

$2\frac{1}{2}$ yards = ? feet

$2\frac{1}{2} \times \boxed{} = \boxed{}$

So, $2\frac{1}{2}$ yards = $\boxed{}$ feet.

1. The distance from Kerry's house to school is 7 miles. What is the distance from Kerry's house to school in feet?

   A 84 feet
   B 252 feet
   C 12,320 feet
   D 36,960 feet

2. Which of the following statements is true?

   A 3 yards > 12 feet
   B 12 feet > 120 inches
   C 1 mile < 5,000 feet
   D 2,500 yards < 1 mile

Practice 2

Julia bought a bag of oranges. The scale showed that the bag weighed 52 ounces. How many pounds did the bag weigh?

What I Already Know	The bag of oranges weighs 52 ounces. The measurement needs to be in pounds.
What I Need to Find Out	How many pounds are in 52 ounces?
What I Need to Do	Convert 52 ounces to pounds.

Since pounds are larger than ounces, use division to convert the measurement.

Complete the problem below.

52 ounces = ? pounds

52 ÷ ☐ = ☐

So, 52 ounces = ☐ pounds.

> Show the remainder as a fraction or a decimal.

---

1. A large vehicle weighs 4,000 pounds. How many tons does it weigh?

   A 1 ton

   B 2 tons

   C 4 tons

   D 10 tons

2. 5 lb ☐ 60 oz

Which symbol makes the statement above true?

   A =

   B >

   C <

   D +

Practice 3

Renee poured 38 glasses of punch for a party. Each glass held 1 cup of punch. How many gallons of punch did Renee need to fill all of the glasses?

Reread the problem to see what you need to do.

You need to find out how many gallons are equal to 38 cups. That means you should convert cups to gallons.

How can you convert cups to gallons?

You should first think, are cups smaller or larger than gallons? Since they are smaller, you should identify that you are changing a smaller unit to a larger unit. This means that you will use division.

What is the conversion from cups to gallons?

☐ cups = 1 gallon

Solve the problem.

$$16\overline{)38}^{\quad R}$$

The remainder shows the number of cups left over.

So, how can you complete this statement?

38 cups = ☐ gallons ☐ cups

---

1. How many fluid ounces are in 5 pints? _____

2. Write in numbers to complete the statement below.

   10 cups = ☐ quarts ☐ pints

Guided Instruction 2

LESSON

6

Converting
Measurements

M5N3.b.   Compare one unit to another within a single system of measurement (e.g., 1 quart = 2 pints).

To convert **metric units** of measure, you will multiply and divide using **powers of ten**.

Convert 242 millimeters to centimeters.

Think About It

Use a conversion table to help you convert millimeters to centimeters.

Metric Units of **Length**
1 centimeter (cm) = 10 millimeters (mm)
1 meter (m) = 100 cm = 1,000 mm
1 kilometer (km) = 1,000 m

The table shows that 10 millimeters = 1 centimeter.

242 millimeters = ? centimeters

242 ÷ 10 = 24.2

So, 242 millimeters = 24.2 centimeters.

> Remember: Divide to convert from a smaller unit to a larger unit.

Try This Strategy

Move the Decimal Point

8,500 mL = ☐ L

What number completes the number sentence above?

1,000 mL = 1 L, so move the decimal point 3 places to the left.

8.500.

Metric Units of **Capacity**
1 centiliter (cL) = 10 milliliters (mL)
1 liter (L) = 100 cL = 1,000 mL

When converting from larger metric units to smaller metric units, move the decimal point to the right.

Study the problem. Use the Math Guide for tips that can help you understand how to convert metric units of mass.

 Math Guide

7.3 grams = ☐ kilograms

What number completes the statement above?

Read the prefixes in the table carefully.

Be sure to find the correct conversion.

Metric Units of **Mass**
1 centigram (cg) = 10 milligrams (mg)
1 gram (g) = 1,000 mg
1 kilogram (kg) = 1,000 g
1 metric ton (t) = 1,000 kg

Use 1,000 grams = 1 kilogram for your conversion.

Way 1: Divide

7.3 grams = ? kilograms
7.3 ÷ 1,000 = 0.0073
So, 7.3 grams = 0.0073 kilograms.

When you convert from smaller to larger units, move the decimal to the left.

Way 2: Move the Decimal Point

0.007.3

You can always use Way 1 to check Way 2 or vice versa.

Now, use what you already know and what you learned to convert metric measurements.

Answer the questions on the next page.

Practice the Skill 2

M5N3.b.   Compare one unit to another within a single system of measurement (e.g., 1 quart = 2 pints).

Choose the correct answer.

1. How many kilograms are in 3.5 metric tons?

   A 0.0035 kilograms

   B 0.35 kilograms

   C 35 kilograms

   D 3,500 kilograms

2. 153 cm = ☐ m

   Which number makes the sentence above true?

   A 1.53

   B 15.3

   C 153

   D 1,530

3. An adult should drink about 2.4 L of water per day. How many milliliters of water should an adult drink per day?

   A 0.24 milliliters

   B 24 milliliters

   C 240 milliliters

   D 2,400 milliliters

4. 6,000 g ☐ 6 kg

   Which symbol makes the statement above true?

   A =

   B >

   C <

   D ≤

5. Compare 5 kg and 50 cg. Which statement is true?

   A 5 kg = 50 cg

   B 5 kg > 50 cg

   C 5 kg < 50 cg

   D 5 kg ≤ 50 cg

6. 8.2 cL = ☐ L

   Which number makes the sentence above true?

   A 0.0082

   B 0.082

   C 0.82

   D 82.0

World Record Road Train

Clifton, Australia—Hundreds of people watched as truck driver John Atkinson attempted to pull the longest road train ever, to break a world record.

The previous record was 117 trailers that were 1,445 meters in length. To break the world record, Atkinson had to pull a longer road train more than 100 meters using a single engine!

On the day of the event, Atkinson had planned to pull 120 trailers that were 1,700 meters in length. But only 112 trailers were usable. Luckily, the length of the trailers was 1,474.3 meters long—longer than the road train used for the previous world record.

Bystanders cheered for Atkinson as he pulled the road train the required distance and broke the world record!

Solve It

Answer each question. Show your work on a separate sheet of paper.

1. Atkinson's road train was 1,474.3 meters long. How many kilometers long was his road train?

2. How many centimeters did Atkinson have to pull the road train to break the world record?

Show What You Learned

M5N3.b.   Compare one unit to another within a single system of measurement (e.g., 1 quart = 2 pints).

Now that you have practiced converting customary measurements and metric measurements, take this quiz to show what you learned. Choose the letter of the correct answer for each problem.

1. 42 in. = ☐ ft

Which makes the sentence above true?

A $2\frac{1}{2}$

B $3\frac{1}{2}$

C $4\frac{2}{5}$

D $5\frac{2}{5}$

2. A water bottle holds 1,500 milliliters of water. How many liters of water does it hold?

A 0.15 liter

B 1.5 liters

C 15 liters

D 150 liters

3. 1.97 kg = ☐ g

Which number makes the sentence above true?

A 0.197

B 19.7

C 197

D 1,970

4. A grocery receives a shipment of 25 gallons of skim milk. How many cups of skim milk is equivalent to that amount?

A 400 cups

B 300 cups

C 200 cups

D 100 cups

5. A loaf of bread weighs 24 ounces. How many pounds does the loaf of bread weigh?

A $2\frac{1}{2}$ pounds

B 2 pounds

C $1\frac{1}{2}$ pounds

D 1 pound

6. 5.6 m ☐ 56,000 mm

Which symbol makes the statement above true?

A =

B >

C <

D +

7. Jamie ran in a 3.2 kilometer race. How many meters did she run?

A 0.32 meters

B 32 meters

C 320 meters

D 3,200 meters

8. 6.7 T = ☐ lb

Which number makes the sentence above true?

A 13,400

B 6,700

C 1,340

D 670

9. How many kilograms are in 52 grams?

A 0.0052

B 0.052

C 520

D 5,200

10. 3,520 yards ☐ 10,560 feet

Which symbol makes the statement above true?

A =

B >

C <

D +

11. A punch bowl holds 17 cups of punch. Which is equivalent to 17 cups?

A 2 pints 1 cup

B 4 pints 1 cup

C 4 quarts 1 cup

D 2 gallons 1 cup

Show your work on a separate sheet of paper.

12. A juice box contains 32 centiliters of juice. How many milliliters of juice does the juice box contain? Explain how you found your answer.

Show What You Know

M5M1. Students will extend their understanding of area of fundamental geometric plane figures.

Before you begin this lesson on area, answer these questions. Choose the letter of the correct answer for each problem.

1. What is the area of the parallelogram?

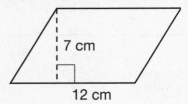

7 cm

12 cm

A 38 cm²

B 42 cm²

C 76 cm²

D 84 cm²

2. The diagram below shows a concrete patio. What is the area covered by the concrete patio?

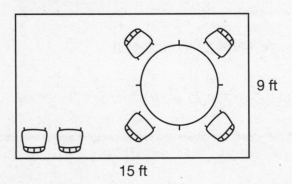

9 ft

15 ft

A 135 ft²

B 67.5 ft²

C 48 ft²

D 24 ft²

3. What is the area of the triangle?

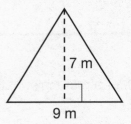

7 m

9 m

A 63 m²

B 31.5 m²

C 25 m²

D 23 m²

4. What is the area of the triangle?

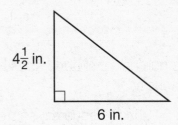

$4\frac{1}{2}$ in.

6 in.

A $10\frac{1}{2}$ in.²

B 12 in.²

C $13\frac{1}{2}$ in.²

D 27 in.²

M5M1.   Students will extend their understanding of area of fundamental geometric plane figures.

When you find **area**, you find the amount of surface enclosed in a closed figure. In Part 1, you will learn how to find the area of rectangles and parallelograms.

What is the area of a rectangle that is 6 cm long and 4 cm wide?

Think About It

You can draw the rectangle on a sheet of grid paper.

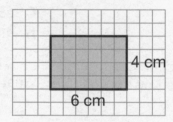

Count the number of shaded squares in the rectangle to find the area of the rectangle.

There are 24 shaded squares, so the area of the rectangle is 24 square centimeters.

Try This Strategy

Use a Formula
What is the area of the garden?

Area = length × width

$A = l \times w$ or $A = lw$

$A = 9\,\text{ft} \times 6\,\text{ft}$

$A = 54$ square feet (ft^2)

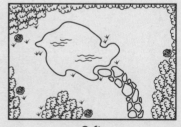

9 ft

6 ft

Study the problem. Use the Math Guide for tips that can help you understand how to find the area of a parallelogram.

 Math Guide

Carefully read the measures of the **height** and **base** of the parallelogram.

What is the area of the parallelogram?

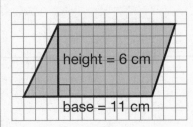

height = 6 cm

base = 11 cm

The diagrams show how to cut and rearrange a parallelogram to form a rectangle.

The formula for area of a parallelogram is like the one for area of a rectangle.

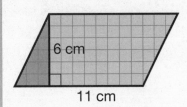 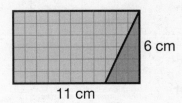

6 cm

11 cm

6 cm

11 cm

You can also write the formula $A = bh$.

Area = base × height

$A = b \times h$

$A = 11$ cm $\times 6$ cm

$A = 66$ square centimeters (cm²)

Area is always measured in square units (units²).

So, the area of the parallelogram is 66 cm².

Now, use what you already know and what you learned to find area of rectangles and parallelograms.

Answer the questions on the next page.

Practice the Skill 1

M5M1. Students will extend their understanding of area of fundamental geometric plane figures.

Practice finding area by solving the problems below.

EXAMPLE

Find the area of the parallelogram.

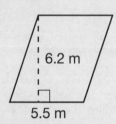

6.2 m

5.5 m

A 3.41 m²

B 11.7 m²

C 23.4 m²

D 34.1 m²

What do you need to find?

Find the area of the parallelogram.

$A = bh$

$A = 5.5 \text{ m} \times 6.2 \text{ m}$

$A = 34.1 \text{ m}^2$

Now, read each question. Circle the letter of the correct answer.

1. What is the area of the rectangle?

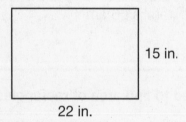

15 in.

22 in.

A 37 in.²

B 60 in.²

C 330 in.²

D 400 in.²

2. What is the area of a parallelogram with these measurements?

$h = 4.70 \text{ ft}$

$b = 3.30 \text{ ft}$

A 5.00 ft²

B 15.51 ft²

C 16.00 ft²

D 17.51 ft²

Sniffing for Mold

Delray Beach, FL—Jada sniffs around a bathroom. She is looking for mold. Mold grows in wet places. It can make people sick. It can grow behind walls where people cannot see it. Jada can find mold with her nose better than technology can.

Months ago, Jada was rescued from a dog shelter. She was trained for 1,000 hours to learn how to smell mold. And not just any mold—she can tell the difference between different types of mold!

Mold sniffing dogs are important working dogs. They help find mold under carpets and in walls. Before mold dogs, people had to drill into walls and rip up carpet looking for mold. Now, dogs like Jada help people save time and money.

Solve It

Imagine you observe a mold dog at work as you answer each question. Show your work on a separate sheet of paper.

1. A mold dog searches for mold under a carpet in a rectangular room. The room is 14 feet long and 12 feet wide. What is the area of the room?

2. A mold dog sniffs in a rectangular area that is 16.5 m long and 13.5 m wide. What is the area that the mold dog sniffs?

LESSON
7
Area

M5M1.   Students will extend their understanding of area of fundamental geometric plane figures.

Review

You have learned how to find the area of rectangles and parallelograms.

Review the methods you can use to find area.

- Count squares on a grid to find the area of a rectangle.
- Use a formula to find the area of a rectangle or a parallelogram.

Practice 1

The community park has a rectangular tetherball court that is 8 yards long and 6 yards wide. What is the area of the tetherball court?

What I Already Know	The tetherball court is 8 yards long and 6 yards wide. It is a rectangle.
What I Need to Find Out	What is the area of the tetherball court?
What I Need to Do	Use a formula to find the area.

Since the tetherball court is a rectangle, use the formula $A = lw$ to find the area.

Complete the problem below.

$A = \boxed{}$ yd $\times \boxed{}$ yd

$A = \boxed{}$ yd^2

What is the area of the tetherball court? _____

1. Monica cut out a rectangle from a piece of paper. The rectangle is 75 mm long and 22 mm wide. What is the area of the rectangle?

    A 97 mm^2

    B 199 mm^2

    C 12,320 mm^2

    D 1,650 mm^2

2. Gavin had a square blanket. The blanket was 8 ft long on each side. What was the area of the blanket?

    A 64 ft^2

    B 60 ft^2

    C 32 ft^2

    D 16 ft^2

Practice 2

Rectangle A is 12 cm long and 7 cm wide. Rectangle B is twice as long and twice as wide as Rectangle A. What is the area of Rectangle B?

What I Already Know	Rectangle A is 12 cm long and 7 cm wide. Rectangle B is twice as long and twice as wide as Rectangle A.
What I Need to Find Out	What is the area of Rectangle B?
What I Need to Do	Find the area of Rectangle B.

This is a multistep problem. First, you need to find the length and width of Rectangle B. Then, you need to find the area of Rectangle B.

To find the length and width of Rectangle B, multiply the length and width of Rectangle A by 2. Complete the statements below.

Length of Rectangle B = 12 cm × 2 = ☐ cm

Width of Rectangle B = 7 cm × 2 = ☐ cm

Now use the area formula to find the area of Rectangle B.

Complete the problem below.

$A = $ ☐ cm × ☐ cm

$A = $ ☐ cm^2

What is the area of Rectangle B? _____

---

1. Rectangle X has a length of 5.2 m and a width of 4.1 m. Rectangle Z is twice as long and twice as wide as Rectangle X. What is the area of Rectangle Z?

   A 18.6 m^2

   B 21.32 m^2

   C 29 m^2

   D 85.28 m^2

2. A parallelogram has a base of 19 mm and a height of 13.2 mm. What is the area of the parallelogram?

   A 501.6 mm^2

   B 250.8 mm^2

   C 64.4 mm^2

   D 32.2 mm^2

Practice 3

What is the area of the **compound figure** shown below?

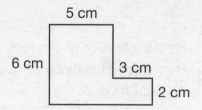

Reread the problem to see what you need to do.

You need to find the area of the compound figure.

How can you find the area of a compound figure?

You can solve the problem by breaking it into simpler parts. The shape is made of 2 rectangles, so you can find the area of each rectangle and then add the 2 areas together.

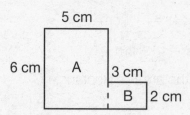

Find the area of Rectangle A.	Find the area of Rectangle B.
$A = l \times w$	$A = l \times w$
$A = \boxed{}$ cm $\times \boxed{}$ cm	$A = \boxed{}$ cm $\times \boxed{}$ cm
$A = \boxed{}$ cm²	$A = \boxed{}$ cm²

Add the two areas to find the total area.

$\boxed{}$ cm² $+$ $\boxed{}$ cm² $=$ $\boxed{}$ cm²

What is the area of the compound figure? _____

How could you check your work?

_____

_____

Guided Instruction 2

M5M1.   Students will extend their understanding of area of fundamental geometric plane figures.

In Part 2, you will learn and apply the formula for finding the area of a **triangle**.

Here's How

What is the area of the triangle shown below?

Think About It

Count the square units on the grid paper to find the area of the triangle.

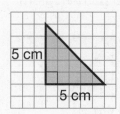

There are 10 squares that are completely shaded.

There are 5 squares that are half shaded. Half of 5 is 2.5.

$10 + 2.5 = 12.5$

So, the area of the triangle is 12.5 cm².

Try This Strategy

Use a Formula
What is the area of the triangle?

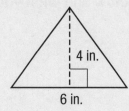

Area $= \frac{1}{2} \times$ base $\times$ height

$A = \frac{1}{2} \times b \times h$

$A = \frac{1}{2} \times 6$ in. $\times 4$ in.

$A = 12$ in.²

Study the problem. Use the Math Guide for tips that can help you understand the formula for area of a triangle.

Math Guide

Carefully read the measures of the **height** and **base** of the triangle.	What is the area of the triangle? 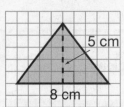
The diagram shows how the area of a triangle is half ($\frac{1}{2}$) the area of a parallelogram.	The formula for area of a triangle is related to the formula for area of a parallelogram. 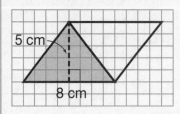
You can also write the formula $A = \frac{1}{2}bh$.	$\text{Area} = \frac{1}{2} \times \text{base} \times \text{height}$ $A = \frac{1}{2} \times b \times h$ $A = \frac{1}{2} \times 8 \text{ cm} \times 5 \text{ cm}$ $A = 20 \text{ square centimeters (cm}^2)$
Area is always measured in square units (units^2).	So, the area of the triangle is 20 cm^2.

Now, use what you already know and what you learned to find area of triangles.

Answer the questions on the next page.

Practice the Skill 2

M5M1.   Students will extend their understanding of area of fundamental geometric plane figures.

Choose the correct answer.

1. What is the area of the triangle?

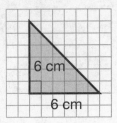

A 12 cm²

B 18 cm²

C 32 cm²

D 36 cm²

2. What is the area of the triangle?

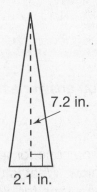

A 15.12 in.²

B 9.3 in.²

C 7.56 in.²

D 5.1 in.²

3. What is the area of the shaded part of the parallelogram?

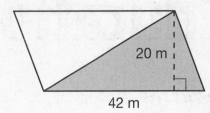

A 420 m²

B 640 m²

C 720 m²

D 840 m²

4. What is the area of the triangle?

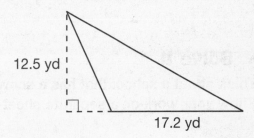

A 215 yd²

B 207.5 yd²

C 122.5 yd²

D 107.5 yd²

NEWS FLASH!

Snowy Education

Lincoln, NH—Students at the Lin-Wood Elementary School bundled up for gym class. Instead of their usual shorts and T-shirts, the students put on snow pants, gloves, hats, and snowshoes.

Many schools in the northeast have added snowshoeing to their physical education programs. Gym teachers wanted to encourage students to go outside, even when it is cold, and saw snowshoeing as a great outdoor activity.

Many students love the opportunity to be outdoors during the school day, even on cold days. The cool air is refreshing, and there is no competition, as with many physical education programs. Gym teachers love the program because it teaches students about a new way to be physically active.

Solve It

Think about a school that has a snowshoeing program as you answer each question. Show your work on a separate sheet of paper.

1. The snowshoe zone for younger students is shown below. What is the area of the snowshoe zone for younger students?

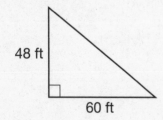

2. The snowshoe zone for older students is shown below. What is the area of the snowshoe zone for older students?

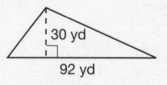

Show What You Learned

M5M1.   Students will extend their understanding of area of fundamental geometric plane figures.

Now that you have practiced finding area, take this quiz to show what you learned. Choose the letter of the correct answer for each problem.

1. What is the area of the parallelogram?

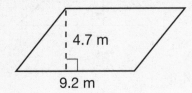

4.7 m

9.2 m

A 43.24 m²

B 27.34 m²

C 21.62 m²

D 13.9 m²

2. The diagram below shows the floor plan for a living room. What is the area of the living room?

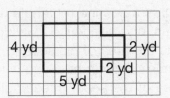

4 yd   2 yd

2 yd

5 yd

A 4 yd²

B 20 yd²

C 22 yd²

D 24 yd²

3. What is the area of the triangle?

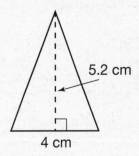

5.2 cm

4 cm

A 9.2 cm²

B 10.4 cm²

C 20.8 cm²

D 41.6 cm²

4. What is the area of the rectangle?

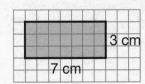

3 cm

7 cm

A 10 cm²

B 20 cm²

C 21 cm²

D 42 cm²

5. What is the area of the shaded part of the parallelogram?

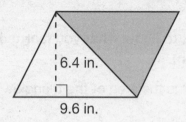

6.4 in.

9.6 in.

A 22.4 in.²

B 30.72 in.²

C 32.0 in.²

D 61.44 in.²

6. What is the area of a parallelogram with these measurements?

$h = 8.4$ ft

$b = 4.5$ ft

A 12.9 ft²

B 18.9 ft²

C 25.8 ft²

D 37.8 ft²

7. The community playground has a sandbox for toddlers to play in. The sandbox is a triangle. What is the area of the sandbox?

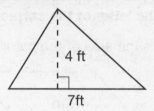

4 ft

7ft

A 14 ft²

B 22 ft²

C 24 ft²

D 28 ft²

Show your work on a separate sheet of paper.

8. Jesse measures a rectangle that is 7.5 m long and 6.25 m wide. He then measures a second rectangle that is twice as long and twice as wide. What is the area of his second rectangle? Explain how you calculate the area of the second rectangle.

Show What You Know

M5A1.   Students will represent and interpret the relationships between quantities algebraically.

Before you begin this lesson on equations, answer these questions.
Choose the letter of the correct answer for each problem.

1. What is the value of m?

    $m + 5 = 20$

    A 4
    B 15
    C 25
    D 100

2. What is the value of y?

    $y - 2.5 = 23$

    A 25.5
    B 25
    C 21.5
    D 20.5

3. What is the value of z?

    $5z = 31.5$

    A 157.5
    B 36.5
    C 26.5
    D 6.3

4. Which operation will you use to find the value of p?

    $p - \frac{4}{5} = \frac{2}{3}$

    A addition
    B subtraction
    C multiplication
    D division

5. For which equation is $a = \frac{1}{2}$ a solution?

    A $\frac{a}{8} = 4$

    B $8a = 4$

    C $8 - a = 4$

    D $4 + a = 8$

6. What is the value of r?

    $2r + 9 = 21$

    A 15
    B 12
    C 6
    D 4

M5A1.   Students will represent and interpret the relationships between quantities algebraically.

When you solve **equations**, you find the value of a **variable** using **inverse operations**. In Part 1, you will learn how to solve addition and subtraction equations.

Here's How

What is the value of b?

$b + 2 = 12$

Think About It

You can use counters to find the value of b.

Take 2 counters away from *both sides* of the equation.

The variable b is equal to the number of counters left on the right side of the equal sign.

So, $b = 10$.

Check your **solution** by substituting 10 for b in the equation.

$b + 2 = 12$

$10 + 2 = 12$

$12 = 12$

Try This Strategy

Use Inverse Operations

What is the value of r?

$r + 8 = 19$

Subtract 8 from both sides of the equation.

$r + 8 - 8 = 19 - 8$

$r = 11$

So, $r = 11$.

Check your solution.

$r + 8 = 19$

$11 + 8 = 19$

$19 = 19$

Study the problem. Use the Math Guide for tips that can help you understand how to solve subtraction equations.

Math Guide	
The variable is *w*. It represents an unknown number.	What is the value of *w*? $w - 1.15 = 7.52$
Addition is the *inverse operation* of subtraction. Addition undoes subtraction.	Use addition to solve the equation.
Adding the same number to both sides of the equation keeps the equation balanced.	$w - 1.15 + 1.15 = 7.52 + 1.15$ $w = 8.67$
Always check by substituting your solution into the equation.	Check by substituting 8.67 for *w*. $w - 1.15 = 7.52$ $8.67 - 1.15 = 7.52$ $7.52 = 7.52$ So, $w = 8.67$.

Now use what you already know and what you learned to solve addition and subtraction equations.

Answer the questions on the next page.

Practice the Skill 1

M5A1.   Students will represent and interpret the relationships between quantities algebraically.

Practice solving equations by solving the problems below.

EXAMPLE	**What do you need to find?**
What is the value of h?	Find the value of h using inverse operations.
$h - 1\frac{1}{4} = 9\frac{1}{2}$	$h - 1\frac{1}{4} = 9\frac{1}{2}$
A $10\frac{3}{4}$	$h - 1\frac{1}{4} + 1\frac{1}{4} = 9\frac{1}{2} + 1\frac{1}{4}$
B $10\frac{1}{4}$	$h = 10\frac{3}{4}$
C $8\frac{1}{2}$	
D $8\frac{1}{4}$	

Now read each question. Circle the letter of the correct answer.

1. What is the value of s?

$16 = s + 12$

A 4

B 12

C 16

D 28

2. What is the value of x?

$x - 2.5 = 8.2$

A 5.7

B 8.2

C 10.7

D 13.2

3. What is the value of c?

$c + \frac{1}{2} = 3\frac{1}{2}$

A $2\frac{1}{2}$

B 3

C $3\frac{1}{2}$

D 4

4. For which equation is $k = 9$ a solution?

A $9 - k = 9$

B $9 + k = 0$

C $0 - k = 9$

D $k + 0 = 9$

| Tyler | Grant | McKinley | Kennedy | Harrison | Madison | Reagan |

Presidential Names

Lubbock, TX—The seven Scheppler children have theme names. Tyler, Grant, McKinley, Kennedy, Harrison, Madison, and Regan all share their names with presidents. Regan's name is not spelled the same, but it sounds the same, as President Reagan.

The Scheppler children all love history because of their names.

Sometimes, homework assignments even teach the children more about their names. Harrison had to read about the Declaration of Independence. During his reading, he learned that President Harrison signed the Declaration of Independence before he was president.

Solve It

Answer each question. Show your work on a separate sheet of paper.

1. The equation below represents how many boys and girls are in the Scheppler family. The variable *b* represents the number of boys.

$$4 + b = 7$$

How many boys are in the Scheppler family? _____

2. The Schepplers have used the names of 7 presidents. They have not used the names of 35 presidents. Use the equation below to find the total number of presidents (*p*) of the United States.

$$p - 7 = 35$$

How many people have been president of the United States? _____

LADDERS to SUCCESS

LESSON
8
Using Equations

Ladder to Success

M5A1. Students will represent and interpret the relationships between quantities algebraically.

Review

You have learned how to solve addition and subtraction equations.

Review the methods you can use to solve addition and subtraction equations.

- Use counters to find the value of the variable.
- Use inverse operations to find the solution to the equation.

Practice 1

At summer camp, 8 campers go on a nature hike. The remaining 12 campers go on a canoe trip. The equation below represents this situation. The variable t stands for the total number of campers. What is the total number of campers?

$t - 8 = 12$

What I Already Know	8 campers go on a nature hike. 12 campers go on a canoe trip.
What I Need to Find Out	What is the total number of campers?
What I Need to Do	Find the value of t.

Since the equation uses whole numbers, use counters to find the value of t.

$t - \begin{matrix} \circ\circ\circ\circ \\ \circ\circ\circ\circ \end{matrix} = \begin{matrix} \circ\circ\circ\circ \\ \circ\circ\circ\circ \\ \circ\circ\circ\circ \end{matrix}$

Draw to show how to find the value of t. Cross out any counters you do not need. Draw circles to represent counters.

Use your completed drawing to complete the statement.

$t = $ _____

What operation can you use to check your solution? _____

1. What is the value of n?

$n + \frac{2}{5} = 1\frac{4}{5}$

A $\frac{2}{5}$ C $1\frac{2}{5}$

B $1\frac{2}{5}$ D $2\frac{1}{5}$

2. What is the value of p?

$p - 243 = 177$

A 65   C 410

B 310   D 420

Practice 2

The price of a hockey ticket increased by $6.20 this year. This year hockey tickets cost $24.95. How much did a hockey ticket cost last year?

What I Already Know	The cost of hockey tickets increased by $6.20. Tickets now cost $24.95.
What I Need to Find Out	How much did a hockey ticket cost last year?
What I Need to Do	Write and solve an equation.

Write and solve an equation to solve the problem. Let t = cost of a hockey ticket last year.

$t + \$6.20 = \$24.95$

What operation will you use to solve the equation? _____

$t + \$6.20 - \$6.20 = \$24.95 - \$6.20$

$t =$ _____

How much did a hockey ticket cost last year? _____

How can you check your work? _____

_____

---

1. What is the value of z?

$z + 4.2 = 13$

A 8.8

B 16.2

C 17.2

D 21.0

2. What is the value of d?

$d - \frac{1}{8} = 1\frac{1}{4}$

A $\frac{1}{8}$

B $\frac{3}{8}$

C $1\frac{3}{8}$

D $1\frac{1}{8}$

Practice 3

What is the value of *x*?

$12 + x - 2 = 18$

Reread the problem to see what you need to do.

You need to find the value of *x*.

How can you find the value of *x*?

The problem is a two-step equation. You can solve it by first performing one operation and then the other operation.

First, undo the subtraction by using its inverse operation, addition.

$12 + x - 2 = 18$

$12 + x - 2 + 2 = 18 + 2$

$12 + x = 20$

Next, undo the addition by using its inverse operation, subtraction.

Complete the equations below.

$12 + x = 20$

$12 + x - \boxed{} = 20 - \boxed{}$

$x = \boxed{}$

Show how you can check your answer.

---

1. What is the value of *a*?

$20 + a - 3 = 25$

A 22

B 17

C 8

D 2

2. What is the value of *d*?

$17 + d - 3 = 21$

A 3

B 7

C 23

D 26

Guided Instruction 2

M5A1.   Students will represent and interpret the relationships between quantities algebraically.

You will build upon what you learned in Part 1 as you learn to solve multiplication and division equations in Part 2.

What is the value of *y*?

$8y = 96$

Think About It

You can use inverse operations to find the value of *y*.

Remember: $8y$ means the same as $8 \times y$

Multiplication and division are inverse operations, they undo each other. So, you will use division to undo multiplication. Divide both sides of the equation by 8.

$8y = 96$

$\frac{8y}{8} = \frac{96}{8}$

$y = 12$

Check your solution by substituting 12 in the equation for *y*.

$8y = 96$

$8 \times 12 = 96$

$96 = 96$

Try This Strategy

Solve a Division Equation

What is the value of *k*? $\frac{k}{9} = 14$

Multiply both sides of the equation by 9.

$9 \times \frac{k}{9} = 14 \times 9$

$k = 126$

So, *k* = 126.

Check your solution.

$\frac{k}{9} = 14$

$\frac{126}{9} = 14$

$14 = 14$

Study the problem. Use the Math Guide for tips that can help you understand how to solve two-step equations.

 Math Guide

The variable is *s*. It represents an unknown number.

Addition is the *inverse operation* of subtraction. Addition undoes subtraction.

Dividing both sides of the equation by the same number keeps the equation balanced.

Always check by substituting your solution into the equation.

What is the value of *s*?

$$\tfrac{1}{2}s + 5 = 35$$

The equation uses multiplication and addition. You will need to use two steps to find the value of *s*.

First undo the addition by using its inverse operation, subtraction.

$$\tfrac{1}{2}s + 5 - 5 = 35 - 5$$

$$\tfrac{1}{2}s = 30$$

Then, undo the multiplication by using its inverse operation, division.

$$\tfrac{1}{2}s = 30$$

$$\tfrac{1}{2}s \div \tfrac{1}{2} = 30 \div \tfrac{1}{2}$$

$$s = 60$$

Check by substituting 60 for *s*.

$$\tfrac{1}{2}s + 5 = 35$$

$$\tfrac{1}{2} \times 60 + 5 = 35$$

$$30 + 5 = 35$$

$$35 = 35$$

So, *s* = 60.

Now use what you already know and what you learned to solve equations.

Answer the questions on the next page.

Practice the Skill 2

M5A1. Students will represent and interpret the relationships between quantities algebraically.

Choose the correct answer.

1. What is the value of p?

$$3p = 19.2$$

- **A** 6.4
- **B** 16.2
- **C** 22.2
- **D** 57.6

2. What is the value of r?

$$\frac{r}{2} = 15$$

- **A** 7.5
- **B** 17
- **C** 30
- **D** 60

3. Which operation will you use to find the value of x?

$$9x = \frac{4}{5}$$

- **A** addition
- **B** subtraction
- **C** multiplication
- **D** division

4. What is the value of t?

$$4t + 5 = 29$$

- **A** 5
- **B** 6
- **C** 24
- **D** 34

5. For which equation is $m = 2$ a solution?

- **A** $\frac{8}{m} = 4$
- **B** $8m = 4$
- **C** $\frac{m}{8} = 4$
- **D** $8 \times m = 4$

6. What is the value of n?

$$\frac{9}{n} + 3 = 6$$

- **A** 15
- **B** 12
- **C** 6
- **D** 3

NEWS FLASH!

Bionic Body

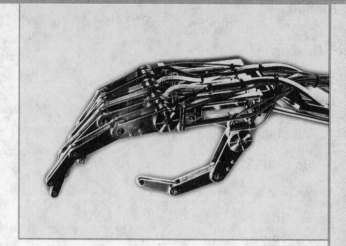

Rome, Italy—Scientists are building a bionic hand that will exchange messages with the brain. Nerves are like tiny wires inside the body sending messages to, and delivering messages from, the brain. Currently, artificial hands are not connected to nerves, so the brain has no control over the movement of the hand.

The new bionic hand, called Cyberhand, will allow the brain to control the movement of the hand. It has a power pack that communicates with the brain. This will allow the Cyberhand to close its fingers around an egg without breaking it or set down a glass after taking a sip of water.

Scientists are also researching how to use the same technology for arms, feet, and legs. In the future, these inventions will improve the lives of patients with artificial body parts.

Solve It

Learn more about the Cyberhand as you answer each question. Show your work on a separate sheet of paper.

1. The equation below represents how many centimeters of wire each of the 5 fingers in the Cyberhand has. How many centimeters are in each finger if each finger has the same amount of wire?

   $5f = 57.5$ cm

2. Each Cyberhand has motors that are used to control the fingers. The scientists have 35 motors, which are enough to build 7 Cyberhands. How many motors are used in each Cyberhand? Use the equation below to help you.

   $7m = 35$

Show What You Learned

M5A1.   Students will represent and interpret the relationships between quantities algebraically.

Now that you have practiced solving equations, take this quiz to show what you learned. Choose the letter of the correct answer for each problem.

1. What is the value of a?

   $8.3 + a = 21.2$

   A 11.5
   B 12.9
   C 23.9
   D 29.5

2. Which operation will you use to find the value of z?

   $\frac{z}{3} = 12$

   A addition
   B subtraction
   C division
   D none of the above

3. What is the value of r?

   $r - \frac{3}{5} = \frac{1}{10}$

   A $\frac{3}{10}$
   B $\frac{2}{5}$
   C $\frac{7}{10}$
   D $\frac{9}{10}$

4. What is the value of k?

   $8k - 3 = 1$

   A $\frac{1}{2}$
   B 1
   C 2
   D 4

5. What is the value of b?

   $7.7b = 24.64$

   A 0.32
   B 1.694
   C 3.2
   D 16.94

6. For which equation is $f = 1.5$ a solution?

   A $7.5f = 5$
   B $5f = 7.5$
   C $\frac{5}{f} = 7.5$
   D $\frac{f}{5} = 7.5$

7. Which operation will you use to find the value of q?

   $8.5 + q = 19.2$

   A addition
   B subtraction
   C multiplication
   D division

8. What is the value of m?

   $\frac{m}{2} = 5$

   A 2.5
   B 3.0
   C 7.0
   D 10.0

9. For which equation is $c = 5$ a solution?

   A $6 \times c = 30$
   B $30 - c = 6$
   C $\frac{6}{c} = 30$
   D $6 + c = 30$

10. What is the value of s?

    $\frac{s}{4} + 6 = 12$

    A 6
    B 9
    C 24
    D 42

11. What is the value of p?

    $\frac{1}{3} + p = \frac{1}{2}$

    A $\frac{1}{8}$
    B $\frac{1}{6}$
    C $\frac{1}{5}$
    D $\frac{1}{4}$

Show your work on a separate sheet of paper.

12. Explain how to find the value of v in the equation $10.5v = 63$. Include in your answer the value of v.

Show What You Know

M5A1.   Students will represent and interpret the relationships between quantities algebraically.

Before you begin this lesson on tables, patterns, and functions, answer these questions. Choose the letter of the correct answer for each problem.

1. Which number is missing from the function table?

$$y = 3x$$

x	1	4	7	10	13
y	3	12	☐	30	39

    A 15

    B 19

    C 21

    D 27

2. A builder plants seedlings to replace the trees he cuts down. He plants 2 seedlings for each tree he cuts down. Which equation can be used to find the total number of seedlings (s) planted if a certain number of trees (t) are cut down?

    A $s = 2t$

    B $s = t - 2$

    C $s = 2 \div t$

    D $s = t + 2$

3. Which equation is shown on the graph?

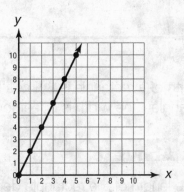

    A $y = 2x + 1$

    B $y = x + 2$

    C $y = x + 1$

    D $y = 2x$

4. During a storm, there are 7 mm of rainfall each hour. Which equation can be used to find the total amount of rainfall during the storm?

    $h =$ number of hours

    $r =$ amount of rainfall

    A $h = 7r$

    B $r = 7h$

    C $h = 7 + r$

    D $r = 7 + h$

Guided Instruction 1

M5A1.   Students will represent and interpret the relationships between quantities algebraically.

You can represent relationships using words, tables, equations, and graphs. In Part 1, you will learn how to show relationships using function tables and equations.

The length of a rectangle is 3 times the width of the rectangle. What is the length of the rectangle if the width is 3 feet long? 4 feet long? 5 feet long?

Think About It

Since the length of the rectangle depends on the width of the rectangle, you can make a **function table** to solve this problem.

Width (ft)	1	2	3	4	5	6
Length (ft)	3	6	9	12	15	18

The length of the rectangle is equal to 3 times the width of the rectangle. This relationship is a **function**.

You can use the information in the function table to solve the problem.

If the rectangle is 3 feet wide, then it is 9 feet long.
If the rectangle is 4 feet wide, then it is 12 feet long.
If the rectangle is 5 feet wide, then it is 15 feet long.

Try This Strategy

Write an Equation

You can also show the relationship between the length and width of the rectangle from the problem above using an equation.

Let w = width of the rectangle, and let l = length of the rectangle: $l = 3 \times w$

Think: The length is equal to 3 *times* the width of the rectangle.

You can also write the equation like this: $l = 3w$

Study the problem. Use the **Math Guide** for tips that can help you understand how to make function tables and write equations to show relationships.

 Math Guide

The cost depends on the weight of the package, so this is a function.

Use letters that represent what the variables stand for. This makes the meaning of the equation easier to understand.

Look for words that give clues about the operations to use in your equation.

Write an equation to describe this situation.

A mailing center charges $3 per box plus $2 per pound to pack and ship a package. How much does it cost to ship a package?

Decide the variables you want to use.

c = total cost to ship a package
p = number of pounds

Translate the words into an expression.

Cost equals $3 *plus* $2 *per* pound

$c = \$3 + \$2p$

So, the situation can be represented as $c = \$3 + \$2p$.

Now use what you already know and what you learned to solve function problems.

 Answer the questions on the next page.

Practice the Skill 1

M5A1. Students will represent and interpret the relationships between quantities algebraically.

Practice working with equations by solving the problems below.

EXAMPLE

A plant starts as a seed and grows 3 cm per week. Which equation can be used to find the height of the plant (h) after a certain number of weeks (w)?

- **A** $w = 3 + h$
- **B** $h = 3 + w$
- **C** $w = 3h$
- **D** $h = 3w$

What do you need to find?

Find an equation that can be used to find the height of the plant.

Write the situation in your own words. Then, write it as an equation.

The height of the plant equals 3 cm times the number of weeks.

$h = 3w$

Now, read each question. Circle the letter of the correct answer.

1. Which number is missing from the function table?

$$b = 3a + 1$$

a	1	2	3	4	5
b	4	7	10	13	?

- **A** 14
- **B** 15
- **C** 16
- **D** 17

2. Jeremy earns $0.05 for each can he recycles. Which equation can be used to find the amount he earns (a) by returning a certain number of cans (c)?

- **A** $a = c + \$0.05$
- **B** $a = \$0.05c$
- **C** $a = \$0.05 \div c$
- **D** $a = c - \$0.05$

3. Which number is missing from the function table?

$$g = 2f - 1$$

f	5	10	15	20	25
g	?	19	29	39	49

- **A** 9
- **B** 15
- **C** 18
- **D** 59

4. In a science experiment, Toby adds 2 grams of powder to each liter of water he uses. Which equation represents this situation?

p = total amount of powder used
w = number of liters of water

- **A** $w = 2 - p$
- **B** $w = p \div 2$
- **C** $p = w + 2$
- **D** $p = 2w$

Herman Melville

Barbra Streisand

John D. Rockefeller

New Yorker Hall of Fame

Woodside, NY—Albert Stern has lived his entire life in New York City. After all the city gave to him, he wanted to give something back. He decided to build a New York City Hall of Fame to honor New Yorkers.

So far, Stern has listed 11 groups of people to honor. These groups include people in health, science, and education. Anybody who is alive or dead may be selected for the new Hall of Fame, as long as they helped improve New York City in some way.

The New York City Hall of Fame is not yet built, but there is already a long list of people to be considered for the hall when it is done.

Solve It

Answer each question. Show your work on a separate sheet of paper.

1. People can be nominated in 11 different groups. Write an equation that shows the total number of people who can be nominated for the New York City Hall of Fame if the same number of people are nominated in each group.

   Let n = total number of people nominated, and let p = number of people in each group.

   _____

2. Imagine that 5 people were nominated who did not fit into one of the 11 categories for the New York City Hall of Fame. How could you rewrite your equation from Part 1 to include these 5 people?

   Let n = total number of people nominated, and let p = number of people in each group.

   _____

LADDERS to SUCCESS

LESSON
9
Tables, Patterns, and Functions

Ladder to Success

M5A1. Students will represent and interpret the relationships between quantities algebraically.

Review

You have learned how to show functions.

Review the methods you can use to show functions.

- Use a function table to show the function.
- Use an equation to show the function.

Practice 1

Anna attaches 1-ounce weights to a spring that is 4 inches long. Each time she adds a 1-ounce weight, the spring stretches another 0.5 inch. How long will the spring be if Anna adds five 1-ounce weights?

What I Already Know	The spring is 4 inches long. It stretches 0.5 inch with each 1-ounce weight attached to it.
What I Need to Find Out	How long will the spring be with five 1-ounce weights?
What I Need to Do	Find the length of the spring.

Since the length of the spring depends on the number of 1-ounce weights, the relationship is a function. You can use a function table.

Complete the function table.

Number of 1-Ounce Weights	0	1	2	3	4	5
Length of Spring (in.)	4.0	4.5	5.0			

Use the function table above to solve problems 1 and 2.

1. How long will the spring be if Anna attaches three 1-ounce weights?

A 5.0 inches   C 5.5 inches

B 6.0 inches   D 6.5 inches

2. The spring is 6.0 inches long. How many 1-ounce weights did Anna attach to the spring?

A 6 weights   C 5 weights

B 4 weights   D 3 weights

Practice 2

It takes Michael 12 minutes to fold a load of laundry. It takes him 5 minutes to make his bed. Write an equation that Michael can use to determine how long it will take him to make his bed and fold a certain number of loads of laundry.

What I Already Know	It takes Michael 12 minutes to fold a load of laundry and 5 minutes to make his bed.
What I Need to Find Out	What equation will represent the situation given?
What I Need to Do	Write an equation.

Since the amount of time depends on the number of loads of laundry, you can write an equation.

Let t = total time, and let l = number of loads of laundry.

Complete the equation below.

Total time equals 12 times the number of loads of laundry plus 5.

↓   ↓   ↓ ↓   ↓   ↓ ↓

___   ___ ___ ___   ___   ___ ___

What equation can Michael use?

_____

1. Jenny has a bag of white marbles and red marbles. For each white marble in the bag, she has 4 red marbles. Write an equation to represent the total number of red marbles (r) in the bag if there are a certain number of white (w) marbles.

_____

2. When a tree is planted, it is 3.2 meters tall. Each year it grows 0.7 of a meter. Write an equation to represent the height of the tree (h) after a certain number of years (y).

_____

Practice 3

Write a situation that could be represented by the equation below.

$y = x \div 5$

Reread the problem to see what you need to do.

You need to describe a situation in words that could be represented by the equation.

How can you write a situation?

Think about what the equation means and then you can write a situation for the equation.

$y = x \div 5$ means a number equals another number divided by 5

Read the situation below.

For a field trip, there needs to be 1 adult for every 5 students. How many adults are needed if 50 students go on the field trip?

Now write your own situation for the equation.

_____

_____

_____

_____

_____

Write two different situations for the equation below.

$a = 2b$

1. _____

_____

2. _____

_____

LESSON
9
Tables, Patterns, and Functions

Guided Instruction 2

M5A1. Students will represent and interpret the relationships between quantities algebraically.

You will build upon what you learned in Part 1 as you learn to graph functions in Part 2.

Here's How

Graph the function represented by the equation below.

$y = 2x + 1$

Think About It

Make a function table. Then, use the values to make a graph.

$y = 2x + 1$

x	y
0	1
1	3
2	5
3	7
4	9

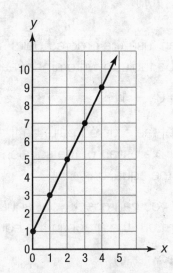

Each *x* and *y* value represents an **ordered pair**. Plot the ordered pairs on the graph. Connect the points with a line.

Try This Strategy

Graph Ordered Pairs

Graph (3,4).

Start at (0,0).
Move *right* 3 units.
Move *up* 4 units.

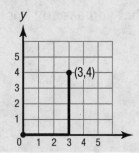

Study the problem. Use the Math Guide for tips that can help you understand how to graph equations.

 Math Guide

What equation is represented by the graph?

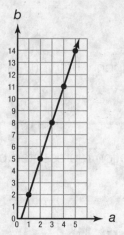

a	b
1	2
2	5
3	8
4	11
5	14

Make a function table showing several ordered pairs on the graph.

Use the graph to make a table showing the ordered pairs on the graph.

Look for a rule that works for all of the pairs in your function table.

Then, use the ordered pairs shown in the table to write an equation.

$b = 3a - 1$

You can choose any ordered pair to check the equation.

All of the ordered pairs on the graph are part of the solution set for the equation.

So, you can check your equation by substituting an ordered pair from the graph in the equation.

Check (2, 5).

$b = 3a - 1$

$5 = 3 \times 2 - 1$

$5 = 5$

Now, use what you already know and what you learned to solve function problems.

Answer the questions on the next page.

Practice the Skill 2

M5A1. Students will represent and interpret the relationships between quantities algebraically.

Choose the correct answer.

1. Which graph represents $d = 15c$?

A d
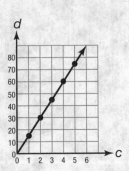

B d
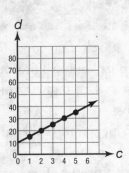

C d
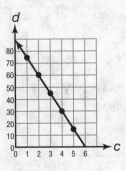

D d
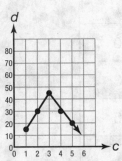

2. Which equation is shown on the graph?

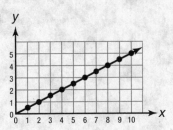

A $y = 2x$

B $y = x - 0.5$

C $y = x + 0.5$

D $y = \frac{1}{2}x$

3. Which ordered pair is part of the solution set for the graph and equation below?

A (0, 0)

B (1, 5)

C (2, 7)

D (3, 5)

Taxing Trash

Oakland, CA—People in Oakland, California, are fed up with fast food wrappers thrown onto the streets. Over 20% of all litter is made up of fast food wrappers, containers, and cups. Cleaning up all of that litter costs cities a lot of money.

The City Council in Oakland decided that enough was enough. They voted to charge a tax to businesses that sell fast food. Most businesses will have to pay only $0.63 per day, or about $230 per year. The highest amount any business will have to pay is $10.45 per day, or about $3,815 per year. Oakland will then use the money from the tax to pay for a clean-up crew to pick up litter. This tax will help make Oakland a cleaner place to live.

Solve It

Imagine you calculate the amount of tax a fast food restaurant has to pay as you complete the problem. Show your graph on a separate sheet of paper.

1. Suppose a fast food restaurant was taxed $3 per day by the city of Oakland. The tax the restaurant has to pay for a certain number of days can be shown by the equation $t = \$3d$ where t = the total tax and d = the number of days. Complete the table. Then, graph the function.

$t = \$3d$

d	t
0	0
1	3
2	6
3	
4	

Show What You Learned

M5A1.   Students will represent and interpret the relationships between quantities algebraically.

Now that you have practiced working with functions, take this quiz to show what you learned. Choose the letter of the correct answer for each problem.

1. Which number is missing from the function table?

$b = a + 3$

a	1	3	5	7	9
b	4	6	8	☐	12

A 9
B 10
C 11
D 12

2. When a seedling is planted, it is 2.5 cm tall. It grows 1.5 cm per week. Which equation can be used to find the height of the seedling (h) after a certain number of weeks (w)?

A $h = 1.5w$
B $h = 2.5w$
C $h = 1.5w + 2.5$
D $h = 2.5w + 1.5$

3. Which equation is shown on the graph?

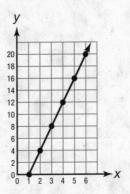

A $y = x - 1$
B $y = 2x - 2$
C $y = 4x$
D $y = 4x - 4$

4. At 3 P.M., the temperature was 72°F. The temperature then fell 4°F each hour. Which equation can be used to find the temperature later that day?

t = temperature
h = number of hours

A $t = 72 - 4h$
B $t = 72h - 4$
C $t = 4h - 72$
D $t = 4h + 72$

5. Which graph represents $d = 2c - 1$?

A

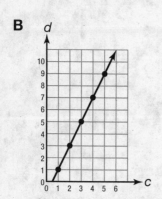

B

C

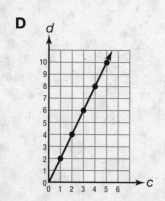

D

6. Which equation is shown on the graph?

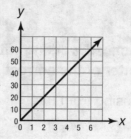

A $x = 10y$

B $x = y + 10$

C $y = 10x$

D $y = x + 10$

Show your work on a separate sheet of paper.

7. Graph the function $y = x - 1$. Then identify 2 ordered pairs that are part of the solution set.

Show What You Know

M5D1.a.   Analyze data presented in a graph.

Before you begin this lesson on line graphs, answer these questions. Choose the letter of the correct answer for each problem.

Use the graph below for problems 1 and 2.

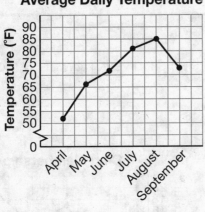

Average Daily Temperature

Use the graph below for problems 3 and 4.

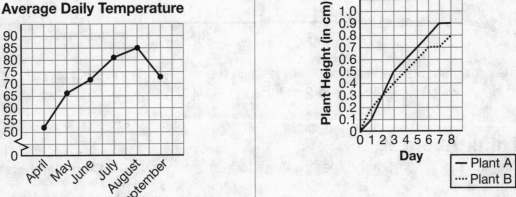

1. What is the average daily temperature in June?

   A 62°F

   B 67°F

   C 72°F

   D 77°F

3. On which day is Plant A shown as having no growth?

   A Day 1

   B Day 2

   C Day 7

   D Day 8

2. Between which two months did the temperature decrease?

   A April to May

   B June to July

   C July to August

   D August to September

4. On which day were Plant A and Plant B the same height?

   A Day 1

   B Day 2

   C Day 4

   D Day 7

Introduction

A **line graph** uses a line to show changes in data. In Part 1, you will study how to read, interpret, and make single-line graphs.

Here's How

The graph shows the number of students in the ski club each year. How many more students were in the ski club in 2006 than in 2004?

Think About It

You can use data from the line graph to solve this problem.

In 2004, there were 17 members of the ski club.

In 2006, there were 19 members of the ski club.

To find out how many more students were in the ski club in 2006 than in 2004, subtract.

$19 - 17 = 2$

So, there were 2 more students in the ski club in 2006 than in 2004.

Try This Strategy

Make Generalizations

In a line graph, the line shows how a quantity changes. Use the graph above to observe these generalizations.

- When the line is horizontal, the quantity does not change.
- When the line rises, the quantity increases.
- When the line falls, the quantity decreases.

Study the problem. Use the Math Guide for tips that can help you understand how to make a line graph.

Math Guide

Since no data occurs before 20°F, draw a jagged line to show the numbers are not left out.

Common intervals to use include by 1s, 2s, 5s, and 10s. Since the temperatures in the data are between 20 and 30, use 1s.

Make sure you are correctly plotting the data.

Check that the axes are labeled and the graph has a title.

Make a line graph using the data in the table.

Temperature at 7 A.M.

Day	Temperature (in °F)
Monday	24
Tuesday	27
Wednesday	21
Thursday	25
Friday	26
Saturday	30
Sunday	25

Temperature at 7 A.M.

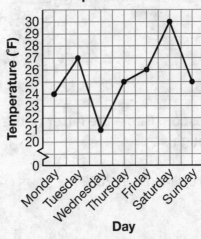

Now use what you already know and what you learned to read and make line graphs.

Answer the questions on the next page.

Practice the Skill 1

M5D1.a.   Analyze data presented in a graph.

Practice reading and interpreting line graphs by solving the problems below.

EXAMPLE

During which year did Isabelle grow 3 inches?

A 2001

B 2003

C 2005

D 2006

What do you need to find?

Use the line graph to find the year that Isabelle grew 3 inches.

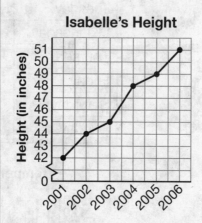

Isabelle's Height

Isabelle grew 3 inches during 2003.

Now read each question. Circle the letter of the correct answer. Use the line graph above for problems 1 through 4.

1. What was Isabelle's height in 2002?

   A 42 inches

   B 43 inches

   C 44 inches

   D 54 inches

2. How many inches did Isabelle grow from 2004 to 2006?

   A 2 inches

   B 3 inches

   C 4 inches

   D 5 inches

3. In which year was Isabelle 49 inches tall?

   A 2001

   B 2003

   C 2004

   D 2005

4. During which year did Isabelle grow the greatest amount?

   A 2001

   B 2002

   C 2003

   D 2005

Storm Ranking

Washington, D.C.—Many people have heard of hurricanes being grouped by their strength. Now, snowstorms will also be grouped using a new system. Snowstorms will be grouped based on size, amount of snow, and the number of people who live in the path of the storm.

Snowstorms will be grouped from 1 to 5. Snowstorms that are in Group 1 will cause some damage. Snowstorms in Group 5 will cause a lot of damage. In the past 100 years, only 2 snowstorms would fall in Group 5.

Many snowstorms will not be grouped at all. If they happen in areas where only a few people live and not much snow falls, they will not be grouped. Most snowstorms that will be grouped will happen around large cities. This is because more people will be affected by snowstorms that hit large cities.

Solve It

Imagine you collect data about snowfall during snowstorms. The table below shows the total amount of snow each hour during a snowstorm. Make a line graph to show the data. Show your work on a separate sheet of paper.

Answer the questions based on your graph.

1. During which hour did the greatest amount of snow fall? _____

2. Between which 2 hours did the amount of snow decrease? _____

Snowfall per Hour

Hour	Snowfall (in cm)
1	2.0
2	4.0
3	6.0
4	7.0
5	5.0

Ladder to Success

M5D1.a.   Analyze data presented in a graph.

Review

You have learned how to read and make line graphs.

Review the steps you can use to read and make line graphs.

- Use data points on a graph to read and interpret line graphs.
- Make line graphs by identifying intervals and plotting points.

Practice 1

During what year was the cost of a movie ticket $9.75?

How can you find what year the cost of a movie ticket was $9.75?

Read the data from the line graph.

First, find $9.75 on the vertical axis (the one that goes up and down).

Then, move across the graph until you find where $9.75 is a point on the graph.

Then, move down to find the year.

During what year was the
cost of a movie ticket $9.75? _____

Movie Ticket Prices

Use the line graph above for problems 1 and 2.

1. During which two years were movie tickets the same price?

   A 2002 and 2003
   B 2003 and 2004
   C 2004 and 2005
   D 2003 and 2005

2. How much did a movie ticket cost in 2002?

   A $8.50
   B $8.75
   C $9.00
   D $9.25

Practice 2

The line graph shows the average speed of a bicyclist. How much did the bicyclist's average speed increase from minute 3 to minute 4?

Average Speed by Minute

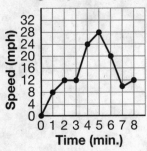

How can you find out the difference in the bicyclist's average speed?

Read and interpret data from the graph.

What is the bicyclist's average speed during minute 3? _____

What is the bicyclist's average speed during minute 4? _____

Now, find the difference between the average speeds.

Average speed during minute 4 − Average speed during minute 3 = Increase in speed

$\downarrow$ $\downarrow$ $\downarrow$

☐   −   ☐   =   ☐

How much did the bicyclist's average speed increase from minute 3 to minute 4?

_____

Use the line graph above for problems 1 and 2.

1. How much did the bicyclist's average speed decrease from minute 5 to minute 7?

A 18 mph

B 16 mph

C 10 mph

D 8 mph

2. What was the difference in the bicyclist's average speed at minute 1 compared to minute 8?

A 2 mph

B 4 mph

C 6 mph

D 10 mph

Ladder to Success *continued*

Practice 3

Gina recorded information from a science experiment in a table. She started to display the data in a line graph but did not complete it. Complete the line graph.

Bean Seedling Height

Day	Height (in cm)
0	0.0
1	0.3
2	0.5
3	0.9
4	1.0
5	1.3
6	1.6
7	1.8

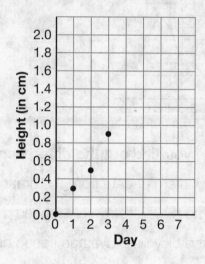

How can you complete the line graph?

First, plot the rest of the data points. When you graph a value that is between 2 quantities on the vertical axis, plot the point exactly between the 2 quantities.

Next, draw a line connecting the points.

Last, give the graph a title.

Use your completed line graph to answer problems 1 and 2.

1. On which day did the bean seedling grow the most? _____

2. How much did the bean seedling grow between Day 2 and Day 5? _____

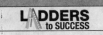

LESSON
10
Reading and Making
Line Graphs

M5D1.a.　　Analyze data presented in a graph.

You will build upon what you learned in Part 1 as you learn to read and interpret **double-line graphs** in Part 2.

Here's How

The graph shows the sales of CD players and MP3 players over the past 7 years at Jenson's Electronics. What were the sales of MP3 players in 2001?

Think About It

You can use the double-line graph to solve this problem.

Read the **key** at the bottom-right corner of the graph. In the key, the solid line shows CD players and the dashed line shows MP3 players. Since the question is about MP3 players, you want to read the dashed line.

In 2001, the total sales of MP3 players were $2,000.

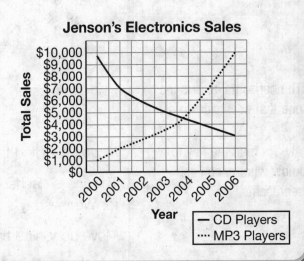

Try This Strategy

Compare and Contrast

When reading a double-line graph, you can compare and contrast the data by looking at the lines of data.

If you look at the double-line graph above, you can tell that as sales of CD players fell, the sales of MP3 players rose.

The point when the solid line and the dashed line cross represents the point when the sales for both CD players and MP3 players was the same.

Study the problem. Use the Math Guide for tips that can help you understand how to read and interpret double-line graphs to solve problems.

 Math Guide

You first read the data from the graph. Then, you will *interpret* it to answer the question.

What is the difference between the high temperature and low temperature on Wednesday?

Weekly High and Low Temperatures

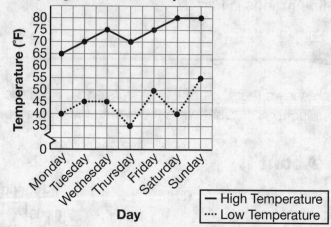

The horizontal axis is the one that goes side-to-side.

Find Wednesday on the horizontal axis.

Always read the key to know what each line represents.

Move up to find the first point. The first point is 45°F.

The line is dashed, so you know this is the low temperature for Wednesday.

Move up to find the second point. The second point is 75°F.

The line is solid, so you know this is the high temperature for Wednesday.

Use the data read from the graph to solve the problem.

Find the difference between the high and low temperatures.

75°F − 45°F = 30°F

So, the difference between the high and low temperatures on Wednesday is 30°F.

Now, use what you already know and what you learned to read and interpret double-line graphs.

Answer the questions on the next page.

LADDERS to SUCCESS

LESSON
10
Reading and Making
Line Graphs

Practice the Skill 2

M5D1.a.   Analyze data presented in a graph.

Choose the correct answer. Use the line graph below for problems 1 through 4.

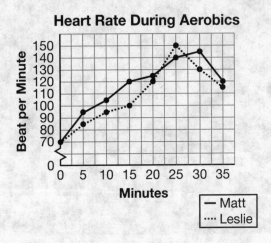

Heart Rate During Aerobics

— Matt
····· Leslie

1. What is Leslie's heart rate after 15 minutes of aerobics?

   A 20 beats per minute

   B 90 beats per minute

   C 100 beats per minute

   D 120 beats per minute

2. What is the difference between Leslie's heart rate and Matt's heart rate after 10 minutes of aerobics?

   A 5 beats per minute

   B 10 beats per minute

   C 20 beats per minute

   D 105 beats per minute

3. During which point is Matt's heart rate lower than Leslie's heart rate?

   A 5 minutes

   B 10 minutes

   C 20 minutes

   D 25 minutes

4. Which statement is true about the data in the double-line graph?

   A Leslie's heart rate is generally lower than Matt's heart rate.

   B Leslie's heart rate is generally higher than Matt's heart rate.

   C Leslie's heart rate is never higher than Matt's heart rate.

   D Leslie's heart rate is always equal to Matt's heart rate.

Mega Solar Systems

Pasadena, CA—NASA scientists have found evidence of 2 mega solar systems. The scientists discovered giant stars surrounded by cloudy discs of planet-forming dust. These cloudy discs are thought to represent planetary systems.

This discovery is surprising to scientists because these mega solar systems are forming around some of the most massive stars known. The stars in the mega solar systems are 30 to 70 times more massive than the Sun!

The discovery was made during a NASA survey of 60 bright stars. The stars in the mega solar systems grabbed the attention of the scientists because of the cloudy discs that suggested planets might exist or form around the stars.

Solve It

The double-line graph shows the temperature readings from two stars over a period of 7 weeks. Use the graph to answer the questions.

1. During week 1, what is the difference in temperature between Star A and Star B?

   _____°K

2. During which 2 weeks did the temperature of Star B remain the same?

   _____

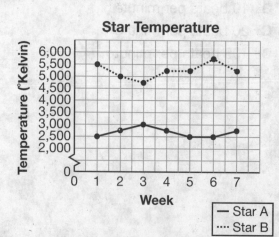

Star Temperature

Show What You Learned

M5D1.a.   Analyze data presented in a graph.

Now that you have practiced reading and making line graphs, take this quiz to show what you learned. Choose the letter of the correct answer for each problem.

Use the graph below for problems 1 through 4.

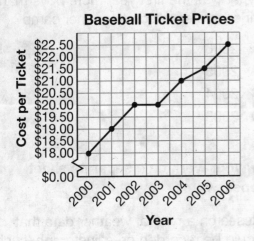

Baseball Ticket Prices

1. How much did 1 baseball ticket cost in 2001?

   A $18.50

   B $19.00

   C $19.50

   D $20.00

2. What is the difference in the price of 1 baseball ticket in 2005 compared to the price of 1 baseball ticket in 2002?

   A $21.50

   B $20.00

   C $2.50

   D $1.50

3. During which 2 years were baseball tickets the same price?

   A 2002 and 2003

   B 2003 and 2004

   C 2001 and 2005

   D 2004 and 2005

4. During which year did 1 baseball ticket cost $21.50?

   A 2003

   B 2004

   C 2005

   D 2006

Use the graph below for problems 5 through 7.

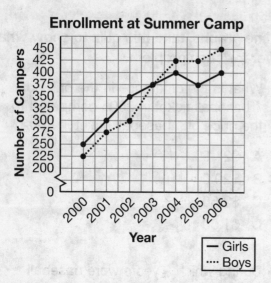

Enrollment at Summer Camp

— Girls
···· Boys

5. During which year were the same number of boys as girls enrolled at summer camp?

A 2003

B 2004

C 2005

D 2006

6. How many more boys than girls were enrolled in summer camp in 2005?

A 25 boys

B 50 boys

C 100 boys

D 200 boys

7. What was the first year more boys than girls were enrolled at summer camp?

A 2006

B 2005

C 2004

D 2003

Show your work on a separate sheet of paper.

8. Research a type of weather data that could be recorded on a line graph, such as average daily temperature or rainfall amounts. Then make a line graph displaying the data. Plot at least 8 points on your line graph.

Glossary

area the measure, in square units, of the interior region of a two-dimensional figure (Lesson 7)

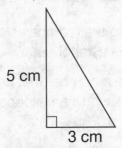

Area = 7.5 square centimeters (cm²)

base of a parallelogram the side of a parallelogram that is perpendicular to the height (Lesson 7)

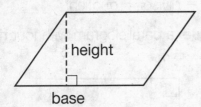

base of a triangle the side of a triangle that is perpendicular to the height (Lesson 7)

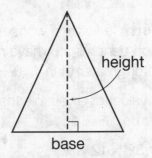

capacity the volume of the inside of a container, often in reference to the measurement of liquid (Lesson 6)

compound figure a figure made from two or more 2-dimensional figures (Lesson 7)

convert to change between units or representations (Lesson 4 and Lesson 6)

customary units units of measure used in the customary system of measurement; units include inch, cup, and pound (Lesson 6)

decimal a number containing a decimal point, such as 1.45 or 0.72 (Lesson 1)

decimal point a dot separating the ones and tenths places in a decimal number (Lesson 1)

denominator the quantity below the bar in a fraction; it identifies the number of equal parts (Lesson 2 and Lesson 3)

dividend a quantity to be divided (Lesson 1)

dividend ÷ divisor = quotient

divisor the quantity by which another quantity is to be divided (Lesson 1)

dividend ÷ divisor = quotient

double-line graph a graph that uses two lines to show the changes in data (Lesson 10)

equation a mathematical statement with an equal sign that shows two expressions are equal (Lesson 8)

equivalent fractions fractions that name the same number (Lesson 2 and Lesson 3)

Examples of equivalent fractions are $\frac{2}{3}$ and $\frac{4}{6}$.

fraction a quantity that names part of a whole or part of a group (Lesson 2)

$$\frac{3}{4} \begin{array}{l}\text{—numerator}\\\text{—denominator}\end{array}$$

function a mathematical relationship in which the value of one quantity depends on the value of another quantity (Lesson 9)

function table a table used to show the relationship between two quantities (Lesson 9)

height the perpendicular distance from a vertex to the opposite side of a plane figure (Lesson 7)

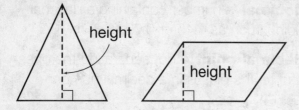

inverse operations operations that undo one another; addition and subtraction are inverse operations; multiplication and division are inverse operations (Lesson 5 and Lesson 8)

key in double-line graphs, a key tells what each type of line stands for (Lesson 10)

least common denominator (LCD) the least whole number that is a multiple of the denominators of two or more fractions (Lesson 3)

length the distance along a line, figure, or object from one point to another (Lesson 6)

line graph a graph that uses at least one line to show the changes in data (Lesson 10)

mass the amount of matter in an object (Lesson 6)

metric units units of measure based on tens, used in the metric system of measurement (Lesson 6)

mixed number a number that contains both a whole number part and a fractional part (Lesson 2 and Lesson 3)

numerator the quantity above the bar in a fraction (Lesson 2 and Lesson 3)

ordered pair a pair of numbers that names a point; an example of an ordered pair is (5, 3) (Lesson 9)

pattern a series of numbers or figures that follows a rule (Lesson 5)

parallelogram a quadrilateral with two pairs of parallel and congruent sides (Lesson 7)

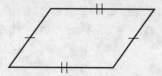

percent a ratio that compares a number to 100 using the % symbol (Lesson 4)

power of ten a number that can be written as 10 raised to an exponent; for example $100 = 10^2$ (Lesson 6)

product the result of multiplication (Lesson 1)

factor × factor = product

quotient the result of division (Lesson 1)

dividend ÷ divisor = quotient

rectangle a parallelogram with four right angles (Lesson 7)

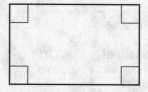

simplest form a fraction whose numerator and denominator have no common factor greater than 1 (Lesson 3)

solution a value for a variable that makes an equation true (Lesson 8)

A solution of $3x = 12$ is $x = 4$.

triangle a three-sided polygon (Lesson 7)

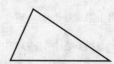

variable a symbol used to represent a number or numbers; in 8x, the variable is x (Lesson 8)

weight a measure of the heaviness of an object (Lesson 6)

Notes

Notes

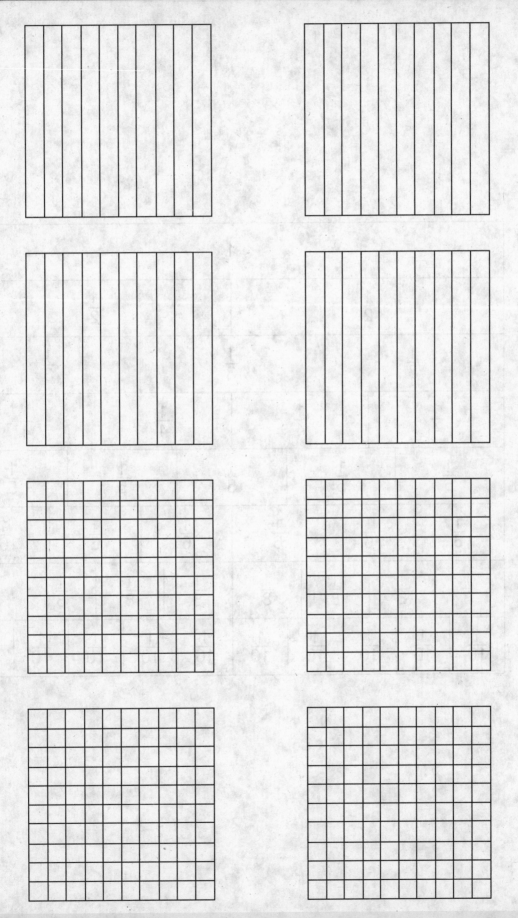

					1					

halves	$\frac{1}{2}$	$\frac{1}{2}$

thirds	$\frac{1}{3}$	$\frac{1}{3}$	$\frac{1}{3}$

fourths	$\frac{1}{4}$	$\frac{1}{4}$	$\frac{1}{4}$	$\frac{1}{4}$

fifths	$\frac{1}{5}$	$\frac{1}{5}$	$\frac{1}{5}$	$\frac{1}{5}$	$\frac{1}{5}$

sixths	$\frac{1}{6}$	$\frac{1}{6}$	$\frac{1}{6}$	$\frac{1}{6}$	$\frac{1}{6}$	$\frac{1}{6}$

eighths	$\frac{1}{8}$	$\frac{1}{8}$	$\frac{1}{8}$	$\frac{1}{8}$	$\frac{1}{8}$	$\frac{1}{8}$	$\frac{1}{8}$	$\frac{1}{8}$

tenths	$\frac{1}{10}$	$\frac{1}{10}$	$\frac{1}{10}$	$\frac{1}{10}$	$\frac{1}{10}$	$\frac{1}{10}$	$\frac{1}{10}$	$\frac{1}{10}$	$\frac{1}{10}$	$\frac{1}{10}$

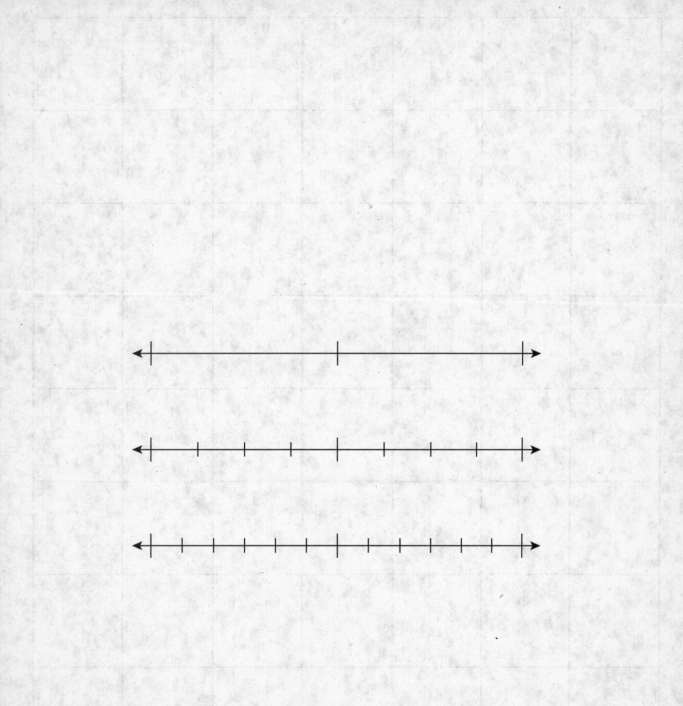

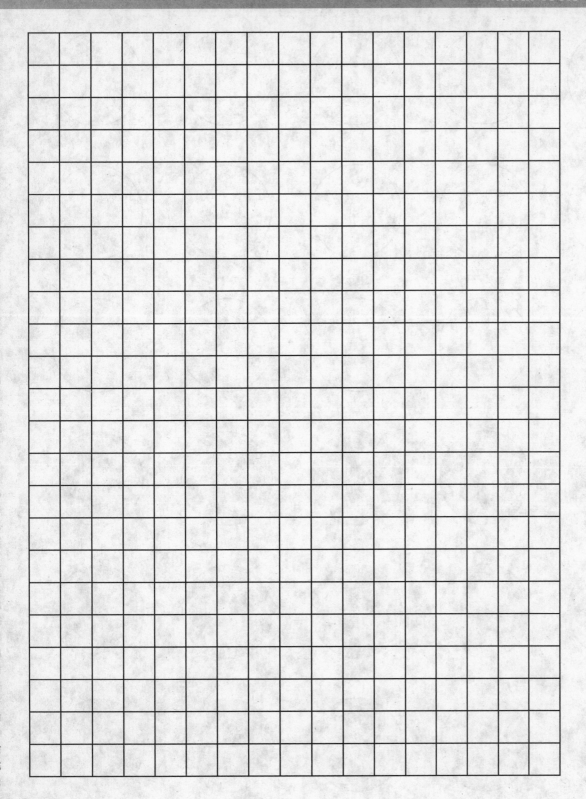

Customary Units	
Length	**Capacity**
12 inches (in.) = 1 foot (ft)	8 fluid ounces (fl oz) = 1 cup (c)
3 ft = 1 yard (yd)	2 c = 1 pint (pt)
36 in. = 1 yd	2 pt = 1 quart (qt)
5,280 ft = 1 mile (mi)	4 qt = 1 gallon (gal)
1,760 yd = 1 mi	
Weight	
16 ounces (oz) = 1 pound (lb)	
2,000 lbs = 1 ton (T)	

Metric Units	
Length	**Capacity**
1,000 millimeters (mm) = 1 meter (m)	1,000 milliliters (mL) = 1 liter (L)
100 centimeters (cm) = 1 m	100 centiliters (cL) = 1 L
10 decimeters (dm) = 1 m	10 deciliters (dL) = 1 L
1,000 m = 1 kilometer (km)	1,000 L = 1 kiloliter (kL)
Mass	
1,000 milligrams (mg) = 1 gram (g)	
100 centigrams (cg) = 1 g	
10 decigrams (dg) = 1 g	
1,000 g = 1 kilogram (kg)	
1,000 kg = 1 metric ton (t)	

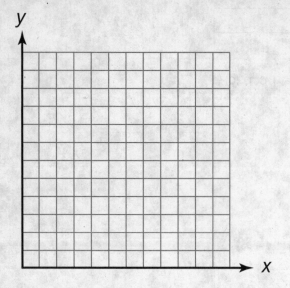

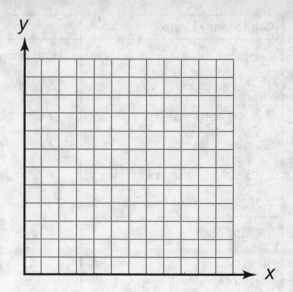

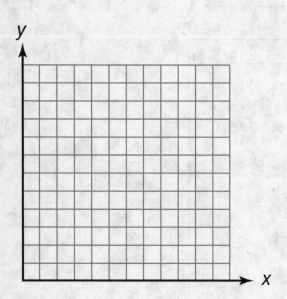

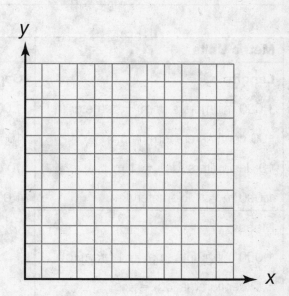

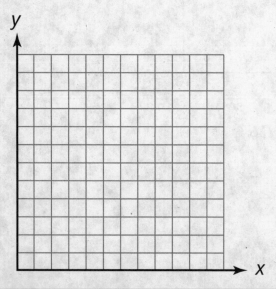

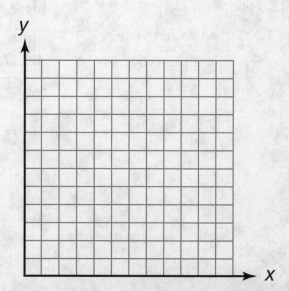